MW01223809

# STRENGTH FOR TODAY
*hope for tomorrow*

Blessings
Dee Kamp

## DEE KAMP
Encouraging Words For All Seasons Of Life

**Strength For Today, Hope For Tomorrow:**
**Encouraging Words for All Seasons Of Life**

Copyright © 2011 Deanne C. Kamp

Published by Forever Books

www.ForeverBooks.ca

for

Grace Every Morning Ministries,

193 Seattle Drive, Port Ludlow, Washington 98365 U.S.A.

ISBN: 978-1-926718-16-3

Printed in Canada

All photographs, stories, and original poetry by Deanne C. Kamp.

Copyright © 2011 Deanne C. Kamp.

Published in association with the consulting agency of WIN Communications/ Writers Information Network, Elaine Wright Colvin, 5359 Ruby Place NE, Bainbridge Island WA 98110

*Helping people to accomplish and to achieve,*
*knowing that their contribution*
*is what God is trying to give the world.*

# Dedication

To my Lord, who revealed to me His story
woven into my stories

To the love of my life, my husband, Bill Kamp

To Howard Lyda, I forever hold you in my heart

To the faithful readers of *His Word,* your encouragement
gave me the courage to write this book

# Contents

# Acknowledgments

I want to thank Elaine Wright Colvin, who helped me with the writing and publishing of this book. Your persistence, perfection, and polishing of each word made it all possible. You were my editor, reminder, and fixer-upper. Thank you for standing beside me until the job got done. Great will be your reward in heaven.

Thank you to each member of my family, my friends near and far, and all my prayer partners. You've been particularly encouraging. God surely blessed me when he put you in my life.

Thank you to my husband, Bill, for the reams of paper you had to buy, for the burned and forgotten meals, for the piles of books you had to step over, and the grace and sense of humor for all the stories I told on us.

# A Word From The Author

This book contains an eclectic assortment of life stories. How can memories of my grandmother's quilt, a little boy and a sandcastle, burly bikers and bees, tumbleweeds, and a skinny kid on a fat tire bike relate to God's Word? What a surprise when I first began writing and collecting my meditations more than four years ago. I never planned to be a writer or write a book.

These fifty-three stories range from my childhood to my grandma-hood. Some are humorous, especially those from the Beaver Valley Country Store which my husband and I owned and operated on the Olympic Peninsula in Washington. After years of working corporate positions in Seattle, we had much to learn about country kindness, generosity, and God's faithfulness through the hard times.

For more than three years, stories kept filling my heart. As I wrote them down, God reminded me of Bible verses revealing He is always with us. I share about the times God picked us up when we fell down, helped us find a path when we were lost, and made us laugh through our tears.

This book is the result of continuing requests for more of these inspirational stories. I pray you will be blessed with strength for your days and great hope for all your tomorrows.

# 1

## God Is My Parachute

W hat are you doing on that ladder in the attic!" my husband called up to me.

"Well, all the kids and grandkids will be here for holiday dinner and I thought it would be fun to drag out these old photo albums. There should be pictures in here to distract some and attract others!" I called back.

With my husband's help, we hauled boxes of photo albums down to the family room and began setting them out. "Now don't start looking in there or we'll be at it all night and never get everything done before they arrive," he said, while pausing to open one album marked *Mexican Vacation 1980*. "Oh my goodness, our grandchildren are never going to believe their grandmother ever did anything as outrageous as this!"

I stared down at the big glossy pictures and began laughing and jumping up and down. "I did that didn't I? Oh my, I forgot all about that part of the trip!" There I was boldly dangling from a parachute flying high over the blue Mexican waters behind a speeding boat! The family all know I'm afraid of heights, and big bodies of water are not one of my comfort zones. I smiled remembering the thrill, the exhilaration of warm wind in my face, the peace and quiet of soaring alone. All my cares were left in the world far below.

I closed my eyes remembering that day so long ago. At just the moment the boat took off and jerked me into the air, I shouted a prayer across the water, "Lord! Be my parachute, and give me a safe and soft landing!"

♫♫♫

*He reached down from on high and took hold of me;*
*he drew me out of deep waters.*
*He brought me out into a spacious place;*
*he rescued me because he delighted in me*
(2 Samuel 22:17, 20 NIV).

♫♫♫

It wasn't the first time God has heard and answered my anxious prayers. As I sailed serenely over the ocean, I recalled how many times God had faithfully been my parachute. I recalled the times when I was in a free fall over an ocean of troubles and sorrows. Through sicknesses, failed marriages, the loss of my only son, transfers, and transitions, God has always been here for me. He brought friends, family, gifts of faith and hope, and His strength to ease me to safe landings. When I couldn't hold on any more, He has held on to me.

Pictures are worth a thousand words, and this one photo was going to allow me tell a story of how once more I called out to God. He increased my courage, changed my fear to faith, and answered my prayer for help.

♫♫♫

"Faith goes up the stairs that love has made
and looks out of the widows
which hope has opened."
—C.Y. Spurgeon

♫♫♫♫

# 2

## *His Helping Hand*

Looking for a safe place to step on the slippery path, we brushed away briars and ducked whipping tree branches. We were blazing a trail to the river where my husband was certain he would find the perfect place to cast his fishing pole and retrieve a trophy fish.

I stumbled along awkwardly through the thick brush, my hands full, not of fishing gear, but a blanket, a book and lemonade in my water bottle. I was going to find that quiet time I had dreamed of all year long.

As I was about to take my next cautious step, my husband suddenly threw his arm out in warning. In a loud whisper he said, "Stop! Don't move—wait, something is coming!"

My heart started to pound. I looked back behind me realizing we had traveled well out of sight of the campground. Had we gone too far for anyone to hear us call for help? That's when I started praying God would give us His helping hand.

♫ ♫ ♫

*"I will lead the blind by ways they have not known,*
*along unfamiliar paths I will guide them;*
*I will turn the darkness into light before them*
*and make the rough places smooth.*
*These are the things I will do;*
*I will not forsake them"*
(Isaiah 42:16 NIV).

♫ ♫ ♫

We had no idea that day in the woods how many more times in our lives my husband and I would be calling to God for help. The future held tough economic down-turns, cancer, death of a child, and more.

Now after all these years, we can confidently share how time after time God has been there when we needed Him the most. He has guided us, been our strength, and the one who lifted us up when we stumbled. Each adventure—from mountain trails to mountains of pain—God has always been faithful.

I held my breath waiting for Bill to finish his sentence. Then he said the craziest thing: "It's a moose!"

"A moose of what?" I whispered back, thinking it must be a huge moose of a bear!

As Bill stepped a little closer to me, he gave me his helping hand to a safe place behind a big tree. Then I saw it—a young bull moose! We watched, not moving or speaking as the tall, stately animal turned to look at us, pause two heart beats, and slowly turn and slip away into the forest.

ʃʃʃ

"Through briars, through waste places, through glades,
up mountain heights, down into valleys I lead.
But ever with the Leadership goes the Helping Hand."
—A. J. Russell, editor (*God Calling*)

ʃʃʃʃ

# 3

## *All I Need For The Job*

We stood side by side outside our Beaver Valley Country Store, sipping hot mugs of coffee in the predawn morning. The air was snapping cold on this late November day. Our son, who was just out of high school, stood beside me dancing from one foot to the other, and blowing on his hands as he waited for his ride.

But he wasn't just dancing from the cold on this morning. His nervous excitement kept him jumping around. It was his first day on a new job. He'd been offered a great opportunity to learn a trade by one of the best homebuilders in the county. A kind man of great reputation and integrity had chosen to hire and teach our son the skills needed to build custom homes.

I watched as my son inspected his new tool belt for the third time. The belt was not equipped with nearly half the tools he would need for this trade, not yet anyway. That would come later.

"Mom, I don't know the first thing about building houses. What will I do if he asks me to do something I don't even know what it is, or how to do it?"

"Son, Hans will never give you a job he doesn't provide you with adequate tools and training for the job. You can count on him. Just listen and do everything he tells you. You can depend on him for all you will need. He is a master at this."

♫ ♫ ♫

*We are confident of all in this because of our great trust in God through Christ. It is not that we think we can do anything of lasting value by ourselves. Our only power and success come from God (2 Corinthians 3:4-5 NLT).*

∫∫∫

As followers of Jesus, we have all the resources we need to be capable and sufficient in anything God calls us to do. What seems overwhelming and we're inadequate in, He provides. Left to ourselves, we often face the reality of our inability to grapple with life. But faith in God supplies what we lack. We have what it takes to build a life on the strong foundation of His promises.

God never gives us a task that He doesn't provide all we need. Through faith and prayer, He provides the tools, the counsel, the training, the wisdom we need to create and navigate our way.

From that day on, our son couldn't wait to go to work. He came home excited to share everything he was learning. To him it was amazing to see a home being built right before his eyes. Every skill, every tool he needed was provided.

By recognizing our weaknesses, we experience God's strength. "God doesn't call the prepared, he prepares the called."

∫∫∫∫

# 4

## A Refreshing, Mysterious Wind

The night seemed to drag on forever in the hot, stifling heat. Tossing and turning for hours I could find no relief. I got up and walked through the dark house. Each step felt as if I was dragging my feet through waves of heat and humidity. I slid open the patio doors and sat in my big overstuffed arm chair—seeking, hoping, for a breeze of relief.

To my surprise a fresh cooling wind blew through the door and whooshed through the rooms. The wind sped past me as if on a mission to seek and overpower all the dry stale air consuming the house. I knew then that prayer had been answered, the weather was changing, and soon rain would follow.

♫ ♫ ♫

*"Just as you can hear the wind but can't tell where it comes from or where it is going, so you can't explain how people are born of the Spirit"* (John 3:8 NLT).

♫ ♫ ♫

Like the refreshing wind coming through the door on a hot night, God's Holy Spirit is able to propel His mysterious wind through our hearts to refresh and renew us. The Holy Spirit has the power to blow away our stale thoughts, stuffy ideas, and dry despairing feelings. When we pray, He will send the Holy Spirit like a wind that lifts the eagle's wings to soar. The Holy Spirit breeze fills us with hope and peace. Call upon the Lord, throw open the shuttered windows of your heart, and invite Him in. Be prepared to feel a mysterious, refreshing wind.

♫♫♫

"And He will raise you up on eagle's wings,
Bear you on the breath of dawn,
Make you shine like the sun,
And hold you in the palm of His hand."
— African Song

♫♫♫♫

# 5

## *Beauty From A Broken Heart*

Digging my way through an old jewelry box, I smiled at what I found. No, it was nothing priceless by market value, like rubies, gold, or silver, but rather one well-worn ring belonging to my grandmother. The silver was tarnished. The stone, an opal, appeared flat and dull looking. I wondered: How could she love opals so much? This one was ugly!

I slipped on the ring and headed for my computer to search the internet for information about opals. I felt I was missing something. I remembered this stone looked so pretty on Grandma's finger.

Opals, I discovered, are made of desert dust, sand, and silica. They owe their beauty not to perfection, but rather to their defects. I read with interest a sentence that made me hold my breath: "The opal is a stone with a broken heart."

The opal is full of minute fissures that allow air inside. Then the air refracts the light. The flaws or fissures create a play of lovely colors, even iridescent. Another sentence in my search made me pause and smile. The opal is often called "the lamp of fire—because the breath of the Lord is in it." Now I understood Grandma's love for this semi-precious stone.

∫∫∫

*To all who mourn in Israel, he will give beauty for ashes,*
*joy instead of mourning, praise instead of despair.*
*For the Lord has planted them like strong and*
*graceful oaks for his own glory* (Isaiah 61:3 NLT).

∫∫∫

The opal on my hand seemed to be changing from milky white to sparkling bits of color. How did that happen? The truth of the opal is it loses its luster if kept in a cold, dark place. But the patina, a soft lovely shine, is restored when it is held in a warm hand or when light shines on it.

In so many ways, I could see the comparison of the opal to us. It is when we are held in His arms and warmed by God's love that we glow with inner beauty and His light to be seen by others. God will use our brokenness, through our defects, to refract a light to the world, enabling us to spread living hope to others. Only God can create beauty from a broken heart.

♫♫

"Without God's touch in our lives—His work in us to will and to do His good pleasure—there is no sparkle or scant joy. But when we allow Him to work within us—when we feel His hand upon us—we are no longer hidden treasures; we become sparkling jewels that beautify His kingdom."
—Barbara Johnson (*Splashes of Joy in the Cesspools of Life*)

♫♫♫♫

# 6

## *The Best Gift List Ever*

W hat on earth can I give Auntie this year?" I asked myself. Ninety-one candles would soon be pressed into her huge birthday cake. Every time I asked if there was something she really wanted or needed, all she would say was: "I need nothing any more. I have all I ever wanted and more than I deserve."

I am not deterred by my aunt's refusal of something special for her birthday, for I have a special gift list given to me a long time ago by my very wise mother.

One day as a young bride and short on funds, I asked my mother to give me gift ideas that would be appreciated but didn't cost much. She searched her desk drawer and pulled out a slip of well-used notebook paper.

Then she said to me, "I call this the best gift ever list. It's perfect for every age, for all occasions. You never have to worry that it won't fit. You'll never have to take it back for a refund."

∬∬

*You must each decide in your heart how much to give.*
*And don't give reluctantly or in response to pressure.*
*"For God loves a person who gives cheerfully."*
*And God will generously provide all you need. Then*
*you will always have everything you need and*
*plenty left over to share with others.*
(2 Corinthians 9:7-8 NLT).

∬∬

I opened the sheet of paper and was surprised at what I read. I thought there would be a list of ideas and where to shop for them. That's not what I found at all. It was a list of gifts one gives of them self.

Generosity reveals that we have been cleansed from a time of self-interest and we are filled with the servant spirit of Jesus himself. An act of generosity is a free gift given at great cost of the giver and a gift that results in giving God the glory.

### The Best Gift List—Ever

- **The gift of time** — spent just for the purpose of simply being with that special someone, no other distractions allowed.
- **The gift of listening** — without interruption or the feeling one must contribute to the conversation, or solve a problem, but in quiet, listen with open and apparent interest.
- **The gift of laughter** — sharing a story, looking at the photo album of happy times that made you laugh until the tears rolled down your cheeks.
- **The gift of a compliment** — being sincere and saying in love and honesty what you admire about the person, in the present and in the past. Write them out one by one to be read and enjoyed later.
- **The gift of hope** — sharing a Scripture verse revealing God's greatest gift, Jesus. His gift of faith and hope and love.

ʃʃʃ

"If the essence of my being has caused a smile
To have appeared upon your face
Or a touch of joy within your heart,
Then in living—I have made my mark."
—Thomas L. Odem, Jr.

ʃʃʃʃ

# 7

## *Be Still!*

"D on't move! Be still!" I heard the mother shout out to her frantic child. On a warm sunny day, three friends and mothers of six preschool children were happily blackberry picking when we were startled by this warning. It was a perfect day for our outing in the woods. Armed with baskets and pails, we selected and assigned each child a spot to begin plucking the huge fragrant berries. We chatted among ourselves, happy to have a break from our normal household chores.

We could hear the laughing and giggling going on as the children were squealing "ouch" from reaching and getting stuck by the thorns. It appeared there was a contest on how many berries made it into the bucket, and how many went into their mouth. The mouths were winning.

With blue smudges around their lips and purple-stained fingers, they were reaching further and further into the thicket for the best berries. Suddenly, the mom noticed little Melissa was not in sight!

♫♫♫

*God is our refuge and strength, always ready to help in times of trouble. "Be still, and know that I am God!"*
(Psalm 46:1, 10 NLT).

♫♫♫

We didn't realize the berries had grown over a large drop-off. Melissa had fallen down a slope. Without thinking about her own safety, Melissa's mother reached down as far into the thicket as she could. She was unable to grab Melissa by the hand. The child was thrashing around frantically, in grave danger of falling further.

"Be still!" the mother commanded loudly.

Everyone got quiet. Not on peep from kids or adults. Not one more word was heard from Melissa.

The command to "be still" must have been difficult for the frightened child to obey, but she had caught the urgency in her mother's voice and obeyed immediately.

Our God is invincible, strong, and able. His arms are long enough, His hands strong enough to pull us out of any sticky situation we find ourselves in. In His Word, God's command to "Be Still" is appropriate and trustworthy. Just like Melissa, we need to listen, stop fussing, and trust God to come to our rescue.

♪♪♪

## BE STILL AND KNOW THAT I AM GOD

God, what does it mean to be still and know You are God?

"My child, what I mean is: Though the earth be removed, though the waters thereof roar and be troubled, though the mountains shake with swelling, though the wind blow, though the storms rage;

IN OTHER WORDS: though your bills are due, though they give you a hard time on your job, though your husband won't act right, though your wife won't act right, tough your children are disobedient, though there's sickness in your body, though your enemies get on your nerves; Stop your WORRYING! Stop your COMPLAINING! Stop your DOUBTING! Stop your FROWNING!

Cease your fears, and dry up those tears! For I'm right here to comfort you, I'm right here to guide you, I'm right here to hold you up, I'm right here to heal you, I'm right here to deliver you. So cast your cares upon me for I care for you. My child this is what I mean by being still And knowing I AM GOD."

—Author Unknown

♪♪♪♪

# 8

# *The Biscuit Quilt*

I have a handmade quilt from the Great Depression. Created by my maternal grandmother, it is made of fabric pieces from old dresses, curtains, dishtowels, and anything else she could scrape together. Each square of fabric was stuffed with cotton and then hand sewn in the shape of a biscuit and then attached and hand-stitched to the quilt's backing. Quilting kept her hands busy and her lap warm in the frigid winters of North Dakota and the harsh times of the depression years.

"I poured out a ton of love and worked out many a problem praying the whole time I was working on the quilt that year," she told me.

♫♫♫

*But each day the LORD pours his unfailing love upon me,*
*and through each night I sing his songs, praying to*
*God who gives me life* (Psalm 42:8 NLT).

♫♫♫

When I was a small child visiting my grandmother, I would always beg for the biscuit quilt. I waited with great anticipation as she dug it out of her trunk. Then she'd spread the lavender scented quilt over me. I felt tucked in and covered with her love.

Grandma knew me pretty well, and knew I often had panic attacks at night. She would smile and say, "Are you sure? It's so big and heavy for you! You won't even be able to turn yourself over! You know dear, a quilt is a great comfort, but it's your prayers to Jesus that will help you sleep."

Grandma was so right. The quilt was too heavy for my little body. I would end up the whole night flat as a pancake unable to move! And she was right too about saying my prayers. Between the blanket of my Grandmother's love and her prayers said over me, I would drift off to sleep feeling loved and secure.

Even now, as an adult I find nights can be long, cold, and daunting with the uncertainty in health, the economy, and more. That's when I remember Grandma's good advice on prayer. It is God I seek for His comforting blanket of peace to ease my anxious heart. And once again, trusting in Him, like the little girl once wrapped in the old biscuit quilt, I rest the whole night through.

*♪♪♪*

A childlike faith shines brightest in a childlike heart.
It's not the absence of fear, but the presence of God
that gives rest to the weary soul.
—Dee Kamp

*♪♪♪♪*

# 9

## *Blind Faith In The Storm*

A rare late spring snowstorm had blown in. As the night wore on, the road in front of our Beaver Valley Country Store was bare of all normal traffic. At ten o'clock at night, those who usually traveled south from the last ferry in Port Townsend had most likely stayed in town. The wind howled and the snow blew in a furious rage by the one weakened light in front of our store. The center and fog lines of the road disappeared. You couldn't see them warning about the deep and dangerous ditches running alongside the roadway.

I was about to close up for the night when I looked out the store window and glimpsed something strange. I could barely believe my eyes. A car was sliding slowly, making its way off the road into our parking lot. The biggest surprise of all—it had no headlights on!

Creeping along, the car made its way close to the front door. The second the car stopped, three doors flew open expelling its passengers. Three women scrambled out, holding onto their hats and scarves, and made their way into the store.

"Where have you come from? And how did you ever make it down that dark road with no headlights?" I asked.

After shaking the snow from their coats and stomping their boots on the rug, the women began hugging and talking all at once. Each was praising God! I left them alone for a moment.

Then I said, "Come on back to the kitchen and get warm. How can we help you?"

"We decided to make it out of town to get home tonight. It wasn't snowing as hard north of here, but halfway down the valley, it became a real storm. Then our car lights went

27

out! We couldn't see a thing. We prayed and prayed asking God to guide us. We were afraid to stop for fear someone else might come along and hit us. We must have been invisible! Our driver was determined, gripped the wheel, and said, 'We're going to make it!' Over and over she said, 'God will guide us!'

"Even though we couldn't see a thing in front of us, she had such courage and faith! It was amazing. We just kept going, depending on the Lord to guide us. Then when we saw your light—we knew we were safe!"

♪ ♪ ♪

*I will bless the LORD who guides me; even at night*
*my heart instructs me. I know the LORD is always with me.*
*I will not be shaken, for he is right beside me*
(Psalm 16:7-8 NLT).

♪ ♪ ♪

Well, I thought, they were surely meant to be here, but now what? Our little apartment above the store didn't have any extra beds. So I sent up a prayer asking the Lord for help. Who could I turn to so late at night?

Just like that, the answer popped into my mind—Jan, our neighbor right up the road. Jan was recently widowed, with a large home she was preparing to turn into a country bed and breakfast. Her house was less than a half-mile away. I knew she wasn't quite ready for guests—but just maybe tonight she would make an exception.

When I called her and shared the dilemma of the three women, she said with enthusiasm, "Bring them on over! I'd love to take them in for the night. Get your husband to drive them over here now!"

With quick phone calls to their families, the women were not only grateful, but also surprised that there was a person who would take them at this late hour, and also have room for all of them! Surely God heard our prayers.

The next morning the sun was out bright and the snow was quickly melting. What a delight to hear the stories of their experience at Jan's house. Plenty of hot cocoa, a warm fire, comfortable beds, and now—a new friend! Jan refused any compensation for the night. It was her delight to have company and the opportunity to help out these stranded women.

How *did* those women find one tiny store on a pitch-dark highway, in a snowstorm with a car that had no headlights? There was only one answer: It was a miracle and one more of God's mysterious ways.

♪♪♪

"Be assured, if you walk with Him,
and look to Him, and expect help from Him,
He will never fail you."
—George Mueller

♪♪♪♪

# 10

## *Bright Hope For Tomorrow*

When my husband was going through radiation and chemotherapy treatments for cancer, he was in danger of not getting enough nourishment. No amount of medication was able to help. He simply needed food to nourish his body. As followers of Christ we find ourselves at risk of being emotionally and spiritually drained by the challenges afflicting our lives.

*∫∫∫*

*My health may fail, and my spirit may grow weak,*
*but God remains the strength of my heart;*
*he is mine forever* (Psalm 73:26 NLT).

*∫∫∫*

These timeless and encouraging words, written by Asph in the Psalms, encourage us even today: God is our strength when all our strength is gone.

We can feed on God's Word to satisfy our greatest spiritual and physical need. When weaknesses afflict us, we can carry on in His name for His love is forever. He promises to never abandon us when we call out to Him.

Whether we struggle in our lives from broken hearts or broken and frail bodies, we can be assured God is with us. Feeding on God's promises is nourishment we can depend on—in our health and in our souls.

My husband was finally sustained and nourished with a special food developed for his immediate need. This special formula enabled him to hang on until the battle going on in his body was over. Today, he shares how it was faith in God's unfailing love that fed his heart giving him strength to hang on. Being nourished daily in God's Word gave him hope and endurance. Today he is able to eat food again and is cancer free, strong, and healthy—a real miracle of God. With God, there is always bright hope.

♪♪♪

"Pardon for sin and a peace that endureth,
Thine own dear presence to cheer and to guide;
Strength for today and bright hope for tomorrow,
Blessings all mine, with ten thousand beside!"
—Thomas O. Chisholm (Great Is Thy Faithfulness, ©1923)

♪♪♪♪

# 11

## *Burly Men And Bees*

One hot summer day at the Beaver Valley Store, my employee and I stood near the old screen door trying to catch a cool breeze. Beaver Valley is traditionally a comfortable place year around, but today was a scorcher. Our two old dogs lay outside under the shade of the porch. Lady, the big black Labrador, was belly up with her paws waving in the air in a rabbit chase dream.

There was no traffic on the two lane country road and the only sound was the bluebottle flies buzzing and banging against the store window. Then the quiet was interrupted by a deep rumble. The roar grew louder by the second. We stretched our necks out the screen door, trying to figure out the noise. Around the corner came a parade of Harley Davidson motorcycles ridden by black leathered men and women.

Our jaws dropped as we watched them stream off the highway. Soon the entire parking lot was filled! A little prickle of fear went through me at first. Are these the good guys? I wondered. I sent up a quick prayer, "Oh, Lord, protect us and give us courage to be good neighbors."

Even more alarming was the sight of these big burly men leaping from their motorcycles jumping up and down, and slapping their bodies from head to foot.

What was this, some weird traditional dance? They were kicking their legs in the air, waving their arms, and yelling like crazy!

Jan and I slowly stepped inside the store. Waiting and wondering what was going to happen next.

A woman ran in the store shouting, "Meat tenderizer! Meat tenderizer! You got some here?"

We stood staring, our eyes wide as saucers, wondering if they were in a hurry to have a big BBQ or something.

♫♫♫

*What good is it, dear brothers and sisters, if you say*
*you have faith but don't show it by your actions?*
*Can that kind of faith save anyone?* (James 2:14 NLT).

♫♫♫

"Bee's, its bees, don't you see? We just rode through a wild swarm of them!"

Jan and I whipped into action. We ran down the aisle of the store and grabbed every bottle of meat tenderizer we could find. Rushing outside we handed them the tenderizer and grabbed the water hose to help make a paste and soothe the pain of those nasty looking stings. After everyone settled down and the bee stomping dance was over, they flooded into our little store buying everything in the deli, the fresh baked goods, and more. All around us were big happy smiles and many heartfelt words of appreciation.

A year passed and the warm summer days rolled around again when we heard the familiar rumble coming down the highway. This time Jan and I only smiled at each other, happy to hear our friends were back. Once again the place filled up with bikers. One particularly big man stood well over six foot tall, looking at us and grinning ear to ear.

What is going on? I wondered.

The big man cleared his throat and everyone got quiet as he announced, "We never forgot what you guys did for us last summer with them bees. And we brought you a little something. Everyone began shouting and cheering, "Beaver Valley, Beaver Valley, Hoorah!"

When the rousing cheer finished, he reached behind him and brought forth a huge stuffed toy—it was a beaver! Something in my heart melted seeing that big burly guy handing me a stuffed toy. I was deeply touched and surprised by the effort they made just to say, "Thank You."

Boy, was I glad that instead of jumping to conclusions that day, we trusted God and jumped into action to help out the best way we could.

∫∫∫

"You will find as you look back upon your life that the moments when you have really lived are the moments when you have done things in the spirit of love."
—Henry Drummond

∫∫∫∫

# 12

## *The Butterfly's Wing*

Light brightens and changes everything. As an amateur photographer, experience has taught me that perfect light will capture the ideal moment in time for eternity. When the clouds climb higher in the sky, when the light of dawn or the glow of a setting sun appears, you want your camera to be near and ready to capture the moment. Light changes quickly and every minute counts. If you look away, it's lost forever.

I casually walked out on our deck to enjoy the first bright sunny day in March. I glanced around the garden, a blaze of yellow and orange flashed among the flowering shrubs. A butterfly!

Dashing indoors, I grabbed the camera and eagerly took several pictures of this flying flower. The sun illuminated the colors on its wings, shifting the patterns from drab to brilliant in a most amazing way. The beauty simply took my breath away.

It was not until later when I printed the photo I realized I caught the butterfly's fragile beauty from underneath its wings! I was at a perfect angle and with a zoom lens was able to see the beauty of the butterfly in a new unique way. The sun penetrating the wings from above revealed a delicate beauty rarely seen when in flight. Now, I have seen how light reflects beauty from both sides.

∫∫∫

*How wonderful to be wise, to analyze and interpret things.*
*Wisdom lights up a person's face,*
*softening its harshness* (Ecclesiastes 8:1 NLT).

*∫∫∫*

Reading the Bible everyday will reveal God's character to enlighten us and ignite us with a beauty that reflects on our faces. Now we can see His light in a new and exciting way. God's Word is the light that creates us to be beautiful in His eyes and lovely to those who see Him reflected in us. The butterfly's true beauty was best seen through the light on its wings from above, so we too are best seen through the light of the love of Christ.

*∫∫∫*

"You will never have a beauty secret
with more visible results
than the study of God's Word.
Let His word evoke your beauty daily."
—Beth Moore (*The Patriarchs*)

*∫∫∫∫∫*

# 13

## Class Five Rapids

When I first began my heartfelt journey to follow Jesus, I thought somehow it would be smooth waters from then on. My river ride to heaven would be in smooth waters, safe and sane. I had no idea there would be class five rapids.

Several years ago, my husband and I went river rafting in the North Cascades. Our guide took a great deal of time preparing us for the trip. He described the type of rapids we'd face on the way to our destination. I was comforted to know this river, in early November, was considered still very low. The river we were about to raft had rapids classed as one and two. I'm a real chicken when it comes to any kind of water, but add rapids and my heart beats louder than the river in a spring runoff.

For my husband, this river was a bit too tame. What is too big to one person is insignificant to others. I was making way too much out of a small rapid that day. That certainly describes my life. I didn't make mountains out of mole hills—I made huge rapids out of mere ripples in a stream.

♫♫♫

*"When you go through deep waters, I will be with you.*
*When you go through rivers of difficulty, you will not drown.*
*For I am the LORD, your God, the Holy One of Israel,*
*your Savior"* (Isaiah 43:2-3 NLT).

♫♫♫

All of us get stuck, lost, and tossed about on our journey to the Promised Land. And what do we do? We panic, we complain, we blame, and we want out of the boat—fast. But the Lord tells us to persevere when we are faced with extraordinary circumstances.

With practical wisdom and clear biblical application, God promises to lead us to a safe place. We are not competent in ourselves, but instead we know we need to depend on God. His grace is sufficient for us and His power is made perfect in our weakness.

Our guide for life is Jesus. He has a plan for our lives and every river rapid is mapped out and known to Him. Our guide in the raft that day told us to watch him, we are reminded to daily keep our eyes on Jesus and not the rapids swirling around us.

Our Lord is knowledgeable regarding what we may encounter on our river ride to heaven. After all, He created the river! He knows of the big bully boulders, and the log jams of life which hinders our progress.

Jesus understands the undertows of discouragement, the sandpits of despair. Jesus sees the twists and turns of our ride that will take us to our final destination. He is in it for the whole ride, and He is there to greet us when we come ashore.

ʃʃʃ

"Faith never knows where it is being led,
but it loves and knows the One who is leading."
—Oswald Chambers

ʃʃʃʃ

# 14

## *Don't Borrow From Tomorrow!*

I'm a professional worrier," my new neighbor recently confessed to me. I discovered this to be sadly true. She is so preoccupied with her worries for tomorrow, she couldn't tell you what is going on around her right now. My grandma use to say, "If you borrow a cup of worry from tomorrow, you'll lose a pound of joy today."

∬∬∬

*Don't worry about anything; instead, pray about everything.*
*Tell God what you need, and thank him for all he has done.*
*Then you will experience God's peace, which exceeds anything*
*we can understand. His peace will guard your hearts and*
*minds as you live in Christ Jesus* (Philippians 4:6-7 NLT).

∬∬∬

When those wild waves of worry worm their way into our heart, we need only to call on the name of Jesus. In one small prayer, big fears are dispelled and will vanish, just as fog is burned away by the power of the sun—in our case, it happens by power of the Son of God.

Spending time reading God's Word reminds us how He really understands our fears. Our Father in heaven wants to replace our fears with joy. With Jesus, we can count on Him to handle all our cares for today and all our fears for tomorrow. Prayer is able to defuse the power of worry, replace it with peace, and fill our heart with contentment. One never needs to borrow trouble from tomorrow again.

∬∬∬

"Said the Robin to the Sparrow:
'I should really like to know
Why these anxious human beings
Rush about and worry so.'
Said the Sparrow to the Robin,
'Friend, I think that it must be,
That they have no heavenly Father,
Such as cares for you and me.'"
—Elizabeth Cheney

♫♫♫♫

# 15

## *Faithful Protector*

Were you ever scared when you were all by yourself, during those times you worked at the store way out here so far from town?" my friend asked me one day. The question made me smile and think back to one occasion that I was indeed watched over and protected.

Before I opened the doors of Beaver Valley Store each day, I would begin with prayer and praise to God for all He had done for us. I was so grateful for His protection over us, for our staff, and our customers. My list of thanksgiving and praise was a long one. Every day there seemed to be one more blessing to be thankful for.

∫∫∫

*If you make the LORD your refuge,*
*if you make the Most High your shelter,*
*no evil will conquer you;*
*no plague will come near your home.*
*For he will order his angels to protect you*
*wherever you go* (Psalm 91:9-11 NLT).

∫∫∫

Seldom did I feel uncomfortable or frightened of people who were new to the area, or who came into the store when I was there alone. For one thing I had my protector who was always with me sitting behind the counter. The protector was Lady, our black Labrador retriever. Lady was the most laid back, happy-go-lucky dog in the entire world. She loved everyone, and never acted the part of protector. It was her size alone that gave the appearance of being a watchdog.

The locals laughed at such a thought. They knew she was just "that store dog" you could find lying upside down with all four legs up. She rarely lifted her head or moved four inches from her favorite spot all day.

One day though, as I was preparing to take the store deposits up to the bank in town, Lady acted out of character. I told my clerk I'd be back soon and headed out the door for my truck. Lady followed as she always did. She loved to ride shotgun on the front seat. Her big adventure of the day was getting a dog biscuit from the teller at the bank drive-through window.

Startled, I felt a tug on the bank bag, and nearly lost my balance, as well as my grip on it. I was dumbfounded to see Lady trying to pull it away. Though a retriever by breeding, that part of the gene pool was never passed on down to Lady. She thought chasing something and bringing it back was utterly stupid. Well, it was not a requirement in order to be our store dog, so we just accepted this and we told everyone we had a un-retriever—retriever!

The next thing I knew, Lady had the bank bag in her mouth and was making a mad dash for the truck!

"Hey, come back here with that! What on earth are you doing?" I called to her impatiently.

When I reached my truck she still had the bank bag and refused to give it up. Every time I reached for it, she turned her head away and even gave me a very uncharacteristic growl!

"Okay, fine. Have it your way," I said, opening the door and letting her jump inside.

It's a half-hour drive to town, but Lady never once dropped the bag. She stared straight ahead, gripping it tightly, refusing to give me eye contact for the entire trip.

When we arrived at the bank drive-up window, Lady more or less just spit out the bank bag onto my lap as if to say, "Now, you can have it. Where's my biscuit?"

It wasn't until I got back to the store later that day that I was to learn why Lady had taken such a fetish for the bank bag.

I didn't pay any attention to a car sitting way back in the parking lot of the store with its engine running. But one of the local men did. He told us later that two strangers just sat watching the store for some time. After I left, they came into

42

the store and were overheard to say, "No use—that big old dog is protecting her."

From that day on Lady always carried the bank bag—I didn't argue one bit. I had a new praise to add to my ever-growing list. I knew, without a doubt, God was watching over us and on that particular day called on one black dog to help me out.

∫∫∫

"Over the years, I've become convinced
that praise sets up a mantle of protection
around the people of God. Praise is an
atmosphere through which
the Adversary cannot move."
—Jack Hayford

∫∫∫∫∫

# 16

## *Five Little Pumpkins*

October in Beaver Valley is a beautiful time of year and this day was no exception. It was a postcard perfect day at the Beaver Valley Country Store. On the wide front porch of the store sat a huge wooden box filled with freshly picked pumpkins just delivered from a local farmer. I could hardly wait for the kids to come and pick out one for the jack-o-lantern-carving contest. We charged only pennies a pound to make certain every family could afford to have one. Soon the porch would be filled with every imaginable decorated, cut, and carved-up pumpkin.

As I stepped into the store, I heard a car pull into the parking lot. I turned to see a station wagon driven by Mrs. Winfred, filled with her five adorable tow-headed boys. The boys were stair-step in age, with the oldest not more than eight-years-old. I always looked forward to these polite and well-behaved children coming into the store. Usually they had a penny for their favorite old-fashioned candy we kept in stock for such thrifty spenders.

But today I was surprised, not one child jumped out of the car when mom got out. They all stayed inside drawing pictures on the steamed-up windows. It was obvious mom was in a big hurry as she ran in the door heading down the aisle grabbing the things she needed. She knew I could see the kids and watch them for her. Something you just did in the country for your neighbors.

♪ ♪ ♪

*The godly walk with integrity; blessed are their children who follow them* (Proverbs 20:7 NLT).

In a flash, mom paid, headed out the door, and was on her way up the road. But in a very short time, I noticed the whole tribe was back. I was curious: What made her return when she was in such a big hurry? That's when I noticed all five little boys come marching through the door, each hugging a pumpkin.

I thought, how cute, five pumpkin-sized kids holding five little pumpkins! "Oh, did you decide to come back and get their pumpkins now instead of later?" I asked.

The eldest boy held up his pumpkin and set it on the counter. His little head was bent way down and his hair flopped over his eyes, hiding what I thought might be a tear coming down his cheek!

"Tell Mrs. Kamp what you did and that you are all very sorry," the mother said sternly.

"What do you mean sorry?" I asked, confused.

"Mrs. Kamp, we thought 'cause the pumpkins were outside all stacked up like ... and, well, we thought they were free! So we jumped out of the car got our pumpkins quick to surprise mom on our way to town. She was pretty mad. We're awfully sorry," he said, barely in a whisper.

The picture before me was so precious, but I dared not smile for I could see an important lesson was going on here.

"Oh, oh, an honest mistake here boys. Thank you for your honesty. You may go out and put them back in the pile now," I said, fighting hard not to laugh out loud.

"You can't imagine my shock when those boys all jumped up in the car and yelled surprise with those pumpkins!" the mother said, shaking her head.

I watched her look after the boys outside as they put their pumpkins in the box. Her eyes held so much love, it made me smile once again.

Those boys are now grown up and hard working men in the community—boys any mother would be proud of. And they have a mother every boy would love and admire.

There isn't a Halloween that doesn't go by that I don't remember those five little pumpkins. I often wonder if the boys still remember their pumpkin pilferage!

♪♪♪♪

# 17

## *Firm Steps Forward*

Now, just hold the ladder still while I climb up," my husband said as he clambered up the ten-foot ladder. I hate holding ladders for people. In those times the absurdity of my ability to prevent a two hundred pound man from falling off makes me weak in the knees. But each year whether it is Christmas lights or cleaning the gutters, my husband puts his faith in me to steady the ladder.

∫∫∫

*I can never escape from your Spirit!*
*I can never get away from your presence!*
*If I go up to heaven, you are there;*
*if I go down to the grave, you are there.*
*If I ride the wings of the morning,*
*if I dwell by the farthest oceans,*
*even there your hand will guide me,*
*and your strength will support me*
(Psalm 139:7-10 NLT).

∫∫∫

Many of us are not confident in climbing a ladder, and less so in holding one up for another. But we can be confident that God has all the strength we need when He asks us to step-up in faith. The Lord will never place us on an unsecured ladder. We can count on Him to be there holding us steady when our confidence is weak, and when we feel we are walking upon shaky ground. With God we can always take a firm step forward.

∫∫∫

"For you, too, there must be songs on the way. Should I plant your feet on an insecure ladder? Its supports may be out of your sight, hidden in the Secret Place of the Most High, but if I have asked you to step on and up firmly—then surely have I secured your ladder."

—A.J. Russell, editor (*God Calling*)

♪♪♪♪

# 18

## *Found In One Old Store*

News of a blizzard in the mid-west made me aware once again of the times when I was a child listening to the stories of my family on the farm in North Dakota. News of a snowstorm always reminds me of a one particular picture hanging in my childhood home. I would stare at the painting for long periods of time and ask my mother over and over again, "Tell me again why the dog is howling in the snowstorm? What happens to the little lamb he's standing by? Will they be all right, mommy?"

Patiently, she would comfort me and say, "Oh yes, they will be found. The shepherd will hear the faithful dog's cries for help and he won't give up looking until he finds them. The dog will not leave the lamb until it is saved. The shepherd won't ever stop looking until he can bring the lamb home to safety again."

Sometimes I could barely bring myself to look at the picture. I felt frustrated that there wasn't more to the painting showing rescue on the way. I didn't understand, but I wanted to believe it with all my heart. How could my mother be so sure? I could never quite feel assured the dog and the lamb were found. As a child, I *was* that lamb lost in the storms of my turbulent childhood.

§ § §

*So Jesus told them this story: "If a man has a hundred sheep*
*and one of them gets lost, what will he do?*
*Won't he leave the ninety-nine others in the wilderness*
*and go to search for the one that is lost until he finds it?*
*And when he has found it, he will joyfully carry*
*it home on his shoulders" (Luke 15:3-5 NLT).*

♪♪♪

Our family moved many times when I was young and misplaced the picture years ago. No one could remember what happened to it. I searched for it in antique shops, collectible places, and yard and estate sales. I wanted to see it again as an adult, as a new believer in Jesus. I wanted to come to peace with it in my heart. I didn't understand why it bothered me so much when I was a child. I *had* to find that picture!

On one hot summer day on a vacation three hundred miles from home, I found myself searching in one more antique store. I kept walking to a storage area way in the back. Things were stashed and cluttered, all piled up as if long-forgotten. I squeezed between stacks of magazines, many old pictures, and empty frames piled to the ceiling. As I was about to turn and make my way back to the main part of the shop, I looked up towards the corner of the ceiling to the very last picture. There it was! After all these years of searching, I couldn't believe I'd found it.

I called to my husband to come quickly! "I've found it! I've found it at last!"

I stood before the painting expecting it to fill me with the same anxious feelings as when I was that little girl so long ago. But it didn't happen. I only felt an odd sense of peace. At first I was confused, until I realized the answer was not in the painting, it was in the story Jesus told in Luke 15. I was no longer that little lost lamb. I had been found by the faithful Shepherd.

My husband startled me back to the present as he declared excitedly, "Is that it? The picture you have always wanted and been searching for all these years? I'll go find the owner and tell him we want to buy it."

As he turned to go, I reached out and grabbed his arm. "No, don't. I don't need it any more. *It* was lost, but now *I'm* found," I said, smiling at the confused look on my husband's face. It's all about the Shepherd leaving ninety-nine sheep to find just one who was a lost lamb—and He found me," I said.

A sigh escaped, relief filled me as I pondered the miracle of it all: Found in one old store, the joy of my salvation and the real secret of the one lost lamb.

♪♪♪♪

# 19

## *Friendship Caught In The Wind*

It was the tough economic times of the late 1960's in Seattle. A billboard said "Will the last person to leave town turn out the lights?" I found myself thanking God for the blessing of being one of the fortunate ones to still have a job. As was normal for my workday, I waited in the predawn hours, along with the other familiar faces, for my bus number 15. Although we were strangers, on this particular cold windy day, we huddled closer together than usual, all our natural social boundaries forgotten. We were like a herd of bison in the city's prairie land. March winds whipped around the tall high-rise buildings with amazing gale force winds, howling so loud you had to shout to be heard.

The cold wind blew through my too thin coat, crept up my sleeves, down my collar, and tugged at my pathetic plastic rain hat. I felt alone and a long way from home. It seemed good times and friends were few and far between.

Finally, we heard the bus splashing its way down the street. Then it slid to a bump against the curb, sending a surprise spray of water on those who stood too close to the curb.

Umbrellas were folded at the top step, newspapers tucked under arms, as the eager group began climbing on board. I shivered as I waited last in line. I was pleasantly surprised when the man in front of me stepped aside to help me up the step and let me board ahead of him.

I turned, giving him a smile and thank you, getting happily on board. I found my regular seat by the window and watched as the man was about to take his first step onto the bus. As he reached for the handrail, a huge gust of wind blew so hard the bus rocked back and forth. I was shocked to see the wind catch his hat and toss it up and over the bench behind him! He quickly stepped off the bus, ran after the hat, and just as he retrieved it—the bus pulled away!

♫♫♫

[Jesus said] *"Here is a simple, rule-of-thumb guide for behavior:*
*Ask yourself what you want people to do for you,*
*then grab the initiative and do it for them"*
(Matthew 7:12 The Message).

♫♫♫

Normally shy and rarely speaking to anyone, I suddenly jumped up and yelled at the top of my lungs to the driver, "Hey! Stop! Wait, you forgot someone! Wait!"

Every head turned to look at me, but I kept on yelling. People stood up and ran to look out the window. The whole bus began to shout, "Stop!"

Oh, I felt so bad. Here this man stepped aside to allow me on first and then this happened to him. At that moment, a most unusual thing happened. It had never been done before that anyone could remember: The bus driver actually stopped the bus in the middle of traffic! He opened the door, and the man with his hat in hand grabbed the handrail and leaped up the steps to a crowd of cheering passengers.

♫♫♫

"Half the joy of life is in the little things taken on the run. Let us run if we must—but let us keep our hearts young and our eyes open that nothing worth our while shall escape us. And everything is worth its while if we only grasp it and its significance."

—C. Victor Cherbuliez

♫♫♫♫

# 20

## *From Start To Finish*

Why unfinished projects seem to be more obvious when the weather turns fair, I don't know. But there they are glaring back at me: books on how to improve my compost for a great garden; more efficient ways to clean and organize my house; seed packets stacked high; paint brushes bristling with opportunities; all those pictures in a box to sort and put away ... many half started projects, never finished.

In my old neighborhood where I grew up, we had a neighbor we called half-finished Eddy. You would find his lawnmower sitting halfway in the middle of the yard. Half the house was painted, half the fence up, and he would spade a patch of land to plant a vegetable garden, but only got it—halfway done. Lucky for Eddy, he had a large and devoted family who all pitched in to give him a hand and pick up where he left off.

We don't need to feel guilty about not finishing everything we have planned. Some things are truly optional. There is nothing wrong if they don't get done. There is, however, one certain race that is essential to finish strong, it is our race of faith.

*♫ ♫ ♫*

*Therefore, since we are surrounded by such a huge crowd*
*of witnesses to the life of faith, let us strip off every weight*
*that slows us down, especially the sin that so easily trips us up.*
*And let us run with endurance the race God has set before us.*
*We do this by keeping our eyes on Jesus, the champion who*
*initates and perfects our faith. Because of the joy awaiting him,*
*he endured the cross, disregarding its shame. Now he is*

*seated in the place of honor beside God's throne*
(Hebrews 12:1-2 NLT).

♪♪♪

In our faith-walk, it's our final steps that are most important. We need to finish strong. And like Eddy, we have someone we can count on to help us, and pick us up when we stall out along the way.

Jesus' best work was his final walk, his last enduring steps to the cross. He held on even when the finish line was the most trying, most difficult of His entire walk on earth.

Let us keep our focus on a strong finish, just like Jesus. Let us keep building our faith muscles by praying, reading God's Word, and giving Him the glory for all that He does to help us along the way. God wants us to win. He wants us to finish well.

Our race in life is never run alone. Just like in a marathon, Jesus runs beside us handing us that cool cup of water, encouraging us, giving us hope to make it through. Oh what a grand and glorious finish it will be! It's not how we begin, it's how we finish that counts.

♪♪♪

"Say not it's a dreadful journey
When the Savior leads the way;
It's but passing through the shadows
To the land of endless day!"
—Bosch

♪♪♪♪

# 21

## *God Provides The Piece*

Thee aren't here!" My husband exclaimed as he crawled on hands and knees across the floor. "Why does this always happen? You get home from the store, faithfully begin your project, you've been promised you have everything you need to put it together, and it never fails — there is one screw or one piece missing!"

I am in the midst of a God-project. All about me are the materials I need for it, my computer has several Google sites saved in Bookmarks, my friends have sent books, as well as sending up prayers. Why then do I hesitate and feel I am not equipped to handle and complete the job?

What "piece" is missing? I search the Bible. In the book of Hebrews I find the "peace" I need in His promise to fully equip me for any situation, project, or circumstance I face.

§ § §

*Now may the God of peace—who brought up from the dead our Lord Jesus, the great Shepherd of the sheep, and ratified an eternal covenant with his blood—may he equip you with all you need for doing his will. May he produce in you though the power of Jesus Christ, every good thing that is pleasing to him. All glory to him forever and ever! Amen*
(Hebrews 13:20-21 NLT).

§ § §

Jesus' death and resurrection so completely reconciled us to God that we can be assured God Himself will prepare us for the work He has called us to do, and then He will see it to completion.

You may be facing a daunting task right now, but be assured: God is for you all the way to the finish.

Is there something missing? Something omitted which is hampering your ability to move forward? Are there more parts than you know what to do with—or too few? More questions than answers? God has promised we already have everything we need! We just need to call on Him and then, in faith—Wait!

One prayer and one quick phone call to the store where our project was purchased and the problem was solved. Though the store was three counties away, we were assured the missing piece was on its way to us that day. We had to wait a bit longer to finish the project, but we were more than satisfied with the results.

We may not see our finished project clearly, but we can rely on God that all the pieces we need are on the way—and they will fit together. When we call on Him, God will always provide the peace we need.

$$\int\int\int\int$$

# 22

## *God Sends Help In Every Storm*

From my office window on the second floor building of this little village, I turned to stare outside at the sudden spring downpour. Sheets of water ran down the sloping parking lot overflowing gutters, umbrellas popped up, and yelps and squeals erupted from shoppers caught in the unexpected shower. I smiled as I watched some of the shoppers take shelter under the colorful awnings of the little shops.

Then I saw her, an elderly woman, shaky and frail. struggling to push open her car door against the rush of rain and wind. She stood up once, but was pushed back into her car by yet another blast of wind and now hail. I feared she would injure herself. Oh no, I thought, stay where you are. This will pass!

But she didn't stay in her car at all. Instead, she made her escape from the car and stood gripping the car's door handle with both hands! She looked confused and frightened, barely able to hang on!

I couldn't take my eyes off of her, expecting she would open an umbrella at any moment and make it to shelter. But I was shocked to see she simply stood there! Her plastic rain hat was slipping off her head, water streaming down her face.

"Oh, Lord," I prayed, "that poor woman—she needs help now!"

∫∫∫

*If you make the LORD your refuge,*
*if you make the Most High your shelter,*
*no evil will conquer you;*
*no plague will come near your home.*

*For he will order his angels*
*to protect you wherever you go.*
*They will hold you up with their hands*
*so you won't even hurt your foot on a stone*
(Psalm 91:9-12 NLT).

♫♫♫

I half expected a shop owner or someone to help her out. But there was no one coming to her aid. Without thinking about my responsibilities to man the desk phones, I jumped out of my swivel chair, grabbed my umbrella, and dashed down the flight of stairs to the outside. I ran to where the woman was standing and without introduction, I popped open my umbrella and held it over her head.

She looked up in surprise and confusion and then gave me the most engaging smile. I linked her arm in mine and just as if we were old friends, I walked her into the candy shop she had been aiming for all along. The store clerk was waiting with the door wide open and said, "Mrs. Stotter, I'm glad you made it!"

"Don't worry girls, I'm fine. Like all storms, this too shall pass," said Mrs. Stotter, with a twinkle in her bright blue eyes. "I'm very glad God sent an angel to help me today. He always sends help in every storm you know."

I laughed at the comment. She thought I was an angel. But I thought perhaps Mrs. Stotter was giving us a very good lesson in faith.

♫♫♫

"Deep faith in action is love,
and love in action is service."
—Mother Teresa

♫♫♫♫

# 23

## *God's Delightful Interruptions*

One beautiful summer morning, my husband and I were on our daily walk. Bill was recovering from his cancer surgery several months before. He was very determined to keep walking and build up his strength again. I was limping along with cranky knees and an arthritic back. We must have looked a sight puffing our way along. In our hearts, we were still that young couple who loved to hike the high trails in the mountains over thirty years ago.

Pausing to catch his breath, I could see he felt like this was a mountain hike, although it was just a small hill on our little country road. We pressed on with little energy to share our thoughts or sing our silly songs as we once did. Today, all our focus was on making it to the top of the hill and back home again

A crunching sound made us lift our heads to see a pretty teenage girl bounding down the hill right for us.

"Hi, I was just coming to see you guys," she said, turning around to walk beside us. This teen is one special girl with a great big heart to help however she can. So many times we were grateful for her cheerful visits during those difficult days when Bill went through chemo and radiation.

"Can I join you then on your walk? Is it okay?" she asked.

I noticed my husband glance my way over the top of her head. Without words I understood what he was thinking: I hope I can make it all the way at her youthful pace!

I smiled back, nodding my head that I understood his concern.

*♫♫♫*

*God is my strong fortress; he has made my way safe.*
*He makes me as surefooted as a deer, leading me safely*
*along the mountain heights* (2 Samuel 22:33-34 NLT).

♫ ♫ ♫

We didn't have to worry. This wise, gracious teen kept to our pace and bridled her youthful energy for the rest of the walk. Her company and conversation lightened our steps and lifted the unseen burden on our hearts. Before we realized it, we found ourselves at the top of the hill and back home again in what seemed like minutes!

Gone was our obsession on how high the hill was, how long the way, or how heavy our burdens. We were so busy listening and sharing that our aches and pains were no longer our focus. We thanked God for sending us this teenager—a most delightful interruption.

♫ ♫ ♫

"Interrupt and enrich your life today
In prayer and praising the Lord.
His Word will lighten each step along the way.
Offer today a warm word to another,
To share along the way
Both of you will be better for it.
It's sure to change burdened steps into play."
—Author Unknown

♫ ♫ ♫ ♫

# 24

## *He Holds The Ticket*

Sometimes the Lord will ask us to leave our country, our people, even our own personal comfort zone. If it's across a continent or across town, when it's in a whole new direction, we can count on God to be with us every step of the journey. God works with a need-to-know plan for our journeys—for each day, hour to hour, and often in the eleventh hour.

My friend Linda often says to me, "God will not give you the ticket to your destination until you are at the train station."

God knows the right time for us to get on board to our destination. He is way ahead of us. He has made the plans and will have the right ticket in time to take us there. All we need to remember is: Be sure and ask Him for it first.

∫∫∫

*The Lord had said to Abram, "Leave your country, your people, and your father's household, and go to the land I will show you.*
*I will make you into a great nation and I will bless you;*
*I will make your name great and you will be a blessing.*
*I will bless those who bless you and whoever curses you*
*I will curse; and all peoples on earth will be*
*blessed through you" (Genesis 12:1-3 NIV).*

∫∫∫

When we are faced with an unknown destination, it is easy to try to work things out on our own without first calling on God. Oh, how we forget God's promises! Abraham found himself in quite a mess one time, being ushered right out of town because he did not trust and consult God first (see Genesis 12).

When with all our hearts we draw close to God with trust and faith, God will draw close to us. He promised! It's guaranteed! Our ticket is ready. It's in His hand. Our destination is planned by the greatest designer, trip planner, and organizer the world has ever known.

♫♫♫

"Upon Thy Word I rest, so strong, so sure;
So full of comfort blest, so sweet, so pure,
Thy Word that changest not, that faileth never!
My King, I rest upon Thy Word forever."
—Frances Ridley Havergal

♫♫♫♫♫

# 25

## *He Leads The Way*

The rolling fog appeared suddenly that early morning we walked along the ocean. It slid low across the tip of the waves, moving deceptively fast toward the shore. We stopped and stared, surprised by the fog's unexpected approach. The sunrise had been some time earlier, bringing a brilliant sun and blue skies for our day at the beach.

The sea was disappearing quickly before our eyes. The fog was on a mission to reach the beach and swallow everything in its path to a gray oblivion, including our path back home.

Never before had I seen fog so low to the earth that you were still able to see the sun shining above it. It not only blotted out ground vision, but muffled all the sounds of the surf, silencing the cry of the gulls. I realized with a flick of fear, we stood in a place between the sea and the land. We could not see either one, but one was creeping up under our feet. The tide was coming in!

I reached for my husband's hand, too afraid to take another step in either direction. "I don't like this one bit. We can't see east from west, land from sea right now," I said.

"Don't worry," my confident husband said. "Your mind is playing tricks on you, causing this fear. We're not far from the path home. It only looks impossible right now, but this type of fog won't last long, just look up! See, the sun is shining right above us. It's stronger and more powerful than the fog and will burn it away soon."

∫∫∫

*You go before me and follow me. You place your hand of blessing on my head. Such knowledge is too wonderful for me,*

*too great for me to understand! I can never escape*
*from your Spirit! I can never get away from*
*your presence!* (Psalm 139:5-7 NLT).

♫♫♫

There will be times when we feel the Lord is far from us. We feel lost with no clear vision of Him. But it's not true at all. Only our fears deceive us. Our Lord is always nearby. We can count on His promise to never leave us or forsake us. The truth of God's Word will clear the fog from our eyes and the fear from our hearts.

My husband was right. Although I felt panicked and wanted to try and run to what I thought was higher ground and the path home, I prayed and kept looking up to the clear blue sky. The light above gave me courage, gave me hope.

"Just like God," I whispered. We waited until the waters were around our ankles. Then as quickly as the fog had come, it suddenly vaporized and disappeared!

There is no fog too dense, no sea too wide or too deep, to keep His love away. We only need to know God is watching over us.

♫♫♫

"You are the One, who leads the way,
The shining truth that lights my day,
You are the peace that fills my soul
That comforts me that make me whole."
—Julie E Jones
(*Psalms of Life by* Salesian Missions)

♫♫♫♫

# 26

## *Hummingbird Surprise*

One sun-filled day, I aimed the garden hose over the bed of roses as usual. I was surprised by a pretty rainbow appearing through the spray. I was lost in thought gazing at the colorful site. Suddenly, a little hummingbird flew out of the lilac tree and zipped in and out of the water, fracturing the rainbow. Can he see the rainbow too, I wondered.

There is a saying, "If it were not for tears, there would be no rainbows in our heart." (author unknown)

♫ ♫ ♫

*Then God said, "I am giving you a sign as evidence*
*of my eternal covenant with you and all living creatures.*
*I have placed my rainbow in the clouds.*
*It is the sign of my permanent promise to you and*
*to all the earth. When I send clouds over the earth,*
*the rainbow will be seen in the clouds, and I will*
*remember my covenant with you and with*
*everything that lives. Never again will there*
*be a flood that will destroy all life"*
(Genesis 9:12-15 NLT).

♫ ♫ ♫

How often when I have felt flooded by my own tears do I rush to wipe them away and go on my own? Rather, I should stop and thank God for all the rainbows He has provided after the storms.

When tears come, it is good to pause and pray. We need to thank God we weren't really washed away in that flash flood of disappointment, sorrow, trials, tribulations. Thankfully, He showers us with rainbows of His love and compassion.

♪♪♪

There is never a teardrop God doesn't see.
His eye is on hummingbirds in the tree.
There is never a storm He doesn't share.
Never a time He doesn't hear our prayer.
Though trials avail, we'll not be overcome,
With Jesus unfailing love, our victories are won!
—Dee Kamp

♪♪♪♪

# 27

## *In The Light Of Day*

In the predawn light, I awkwardly shuffled my inappropriate bedroom slippers down the graveled driveway to the newspaper box. I'm waving my arms wildly. It's throwing the light from my flashlight all over the place but where I need it most. All this craziness is simple to explain, I'm trying to avoid the abundance of spider webs. I will do anything to avoid a dripping dewy wet spider web draping across my face. Spiders are my nemesis! It's that time of year again when they work overtime creating those intricate doilies.

I can only imagine the image I must portray to my neighbor, if she is watching from her house on the hill behind us. I glance quickly over my shoulder hoping not to see any lights on in their kitchen. I laugh at myself, thinking I must look like Don Quixote fighting imaginary windmills.

Returning to the house, the sun is climbing over the mountains, spraying amazing sunbeams across the sky. In just seconds, the night shadows disappear. I can see clearly all around me. Turning off the flashlight, I catch my breath at the sight of my garden.

Dozens of perfectly formed spider webs, that once were scary, are now dazzling and looking more like crystal Christmas lights. God's light has thrown the ordinary web into an extraordinary pallet of art and beauty. The web is so perfectly created, delicately designed for the spider's single purpose, but giving us double pleasure in its exquisiteness. God so often shows Himself to us in the most delightful ways.

*∫∫∫*

*Satisfy us in the morning with your unfailing love,*
*so we may sing for joy to the end of*
*our lives* (Psalm 90:14 NLT).

♫♫♫

I whisper a prayer, "Let me see your miracles again and again, Lord. Open the eyes of my heart to see more of you. Remind me of how you replace sadness with gladness, and change sorrow to songs of joy. Thank you, Lord! We see the works of your hand and know you designed all things for us to enjoy. Help me to be patient and trusting, Lord, knowing everything is in your hands and in your time. As I trust, I find my rest in you."

♫♫♫

"To the heart that is attuned to Him,
God comes in surprising ways."
—Henry Gariepy

♫♫♫♫

# 28

## *It's All In The Pressing*

It was a pressing matter, and the iron was hot! I'm from a generation where we ironed—everything! I have talked to other women whose mother's carried "freshly-ironed" to extremes—they even ironed underwear. In my home, we ironed all the useable, wearable, and practical items.

We were a family of six, and the ironing basket was piled high by ironing day. Sometimes my mother kept the starched shirts in the refrigerator, so they wouldn't mildew. Preparing to iron meant waiting for the iron to get hot and filling the Coke bottle with water fitted with a little sprinkle head used for dampening each piece before pressing. A quick press would never do. Each piece, according to my mother, was worthy of our best time and effort.

*ʃ ʃ ʃ*

*I don't mean to say that I have already achieved these things or that I have already reached perfection.
But I press on to possess that perfection for which Christ Jesus first possessed me. No, dear brothers and sisters, I have not achieved it, but I focus on this one thing: Forgetting the past and looking forward to what lies ahead. I press on to reach the end of the race to receive the heavenly prize for which God, through Christ Jesus, is calling us* (Philippians 3:12-13 NLT).

*ʃ ʃ ʃ*

God has made us of good fabric, His best enduring design. And God can make something beautiful of our lives! All we need to do is give Him the pieces and press in on our faith.

God doesn't rush things, He didn't make us of perm-a-press fabric, to stay wrinkle free for life. He is never satisfied with a quick fix, an easy pressing. He shapes and improves the fabric of our character to be in His beautiful image.

There's no quick fix for our crumpled state. There can be no smoothing over or pressing our way out of things. God doesn't want us to shove the hard things in our life to the bottom of our ironing basket. He wants us to come to Him in prayer. God can handle all the large loads of our un-pressed laundry!

Though our fabric may grow thin and fragile, we can count on "the Grand Weaver" to give us the strength to press on through each difficultly and reach His design for our lives.

♪♪♪

"Take God. Take hold. Move out.
Reach up for the stars.
Let God make something beautiful out of your life."
—James C. Hefley (*Life Changes*)

♪♪♪♪

# 29

## *Let Down Our Wings*

The American Kestrel is a robin-sized bird, sporting beautifully detailed markings of rust and charcoal gray. Though too small to look like a mighty hunter, all mice and small birds know that it truly is one to fear. You may see this little bird hunting in the most unlikely places. One such time for me was when I was in backed-up traffic on the freeway due to nasty winter weather.

Suddenly, the little bird swooped off its perch on the lamp near the freeway and swept over the median. There it seemed to simply stop in midair and begin a series of rapid wing beats. The little bird pulled up and hovered in the sky like a tiny helicopter. With pure concentration on the hunt and the rapid beat of its wings, the Kestrel was oblivious to horns honking, trucks rumbling, and people shouting. When the wings of this little hunter were beating, it heard and saw nothing at all.

∫∫∫

*As they flew, their wings sounded to me like the waves crashing against the shore or like the voice of the Almighty or like the shouting of a mighty army. When they stopped, they let down their wings. As they stood with wings lowered, a voice spoke from beyond the crystal surface above them (Ezekiel 1:24-25 NLT).*

∫∫∫

Ezekiel saw a vision, and in the vision more than one great truth was revealed. But the very last sentence speaks of how they let down their wings and a great voice spoke to them.

When we are calm and in a restful state, it is then we will hear the Lord. Sometimes the answer may be simply to stop fluttering around, to hold off the strong desire to hover too close to our problems, and to simply wait upon Him. To be still and let down our wings is something we rarely do. But until we do, we may miss a sweet message to our soul from our loving Heavenly Father.

♫♫♫

"Be still! Just now be still!
There comes a presence very mild and sweet;
White were the sandals of His noiseless feet.
It is the Comforter whom Jesus sent
To teach you what the words He uttered meant.
The willing, waiting spirit, He does fill.
If you would hear His message,
Dear soul, be still!"
—L. B. Cowman
(*Streams in the Desert*)

♫♫♫♫

# 30

## *Let God Be Our Travel Agent*

Friends are preparing to leave on a long journey, a mission trip to a third world country. I yearn to take a journey, too. But it's not my season for travel, in timing—both physically and spiritually. To travel, teach, and share the Word of God so that others would find Jesus, is a longing in my heart. But God has other travel plans for me, as He does for others, right now. These plans do not require us to take trains, planes, ships, or automobiles.

A journey of the heart doesn't always mean we must travel far away. God is more interested in our journey which leads us closer to His heart, and changes us into the likeness of His Son, Jesus.

∫∫∫

*But thanks be to God, who always leads us in triumphal procession in Christ, and through us spreads everywhere the fragrance of the knowledge of him* (2 Corinthians 2:14 NIV).

∫∫∫

Letting God be our travel agent puts us in step with Jesus. God's travel plans include others to join us, so they too will find Him as their Source for all they need. Let us eagerly book ourselves on the journey of His choice. One in which we will be transformed regardless of the places we go, or the perils we face, or the surprises that pop up, or the ruts in the road which cause all sorts of adversity along our way.

God's invitation often comes as a soft whisper from deep within our heart. A journey with God finds us in peaceful harmony with Him. He will enable us to have the courage it takes to make that leap in faith to the destination of His choice. God is our counselor, tour guide, and our trustworthy travel companion.

He is in every detail of our lives, with us on every journey we face. Our God is in the beginning and He is there to the end of our travels—for this lifetime and on to an eternity with Him.

God desires to transform our lives, our actions, and our attitudes to draw us closer to Him. Obeying God and living for His purpose, according to His plan, in every journey, in all seasons, has the power to change our lives and the lives of others forever.

♫♫♫

All that I need to be
All for the journey ahead of me
All I need is His face to see
All that and more—God provides for me.
—Dee Kamp

♫♫♫♫

# 31

## *Like Tumbleweeds*

The wind blew dust from the prairie so thick it obscured our vision of the highway. I watched the tumbleweeds rolling along and pile up against the fences. But some were being flipped into the air by gusts of wind, rolled out onto the highway, and smacked hard against the motor home. On the radio, the highway patrol warned everyone that tumbleweeds can be dangerous and even life-threatening.

I have seen tourists stop and pick up a tumbleweed and toss it in the back of their car for home decoration. It's the last thing a North Dakota farmer would think of doing. They once thought of fencing the entire state of North Dakota to stop tumbleweeds from causing injury to their horses from the thorns, and from their ability to carry a prairie fire across many acres of farmland.

The tumbleweed grows until its seeds are mature. Then the stem breaks off, allowing this perfect ball of a plant to be tossed by the winds and disperse seeds for miles. Interestingly, science has shown that the plant is so well-created it does not lose all of its seeds on the first bounce, but is designed to let the seeds come loose one bounce at a time. This plant survives because it can bounce in adversity.

ʃ ʃ ʃ

*Dear brothers and sisters, when troubles come*
*Your way, consider it an opportunity for great joy.*
*For you know that when your faith is tested, your*
*endurance has a chance to grow. So let it grow,*

*for when your endurance is fully developed,*
*you will be perfect and complete, needing*
*nothing* (James 1:2-4 NLT).

♪♪♪

The tumbleweed has a lot going for it. Endurance allows it to survive, grow, and disperse its seeds. To some, it is a just a nuisance. But now scientists at Utah State University have found that tumbleweeds improve the soil. Tumbleweeds trickle chemicals into the soil and this improves the nutrients in the ground, so other plants grow better the next season.

Just like the tumbleweed, we are designed with endurance and the bounce to survive. By faith, we are able to disperse seeds of hope, faith, and love. When we roll into the lives of others who live with tired soil in their souls, we are able to nurture them in God's Word, leaving a place where Christ will grow.

♪♪♪

"Thou has made us for Thyself,
And the heart of man is restless
Until it finds its rest in Thee."
—St. Augustine

♪♪♪♪

# 32

## Like A Refreshing Dew

A trip to Northern California to visit our family has us once again driving through the wonderful giant redwoods, the Sequoias. No matter how many times we drive the narrow two lane highway, the majesty of the huge magnificent trees hush all hurried and anxious thoughts. These ancient trees grow more than 300 feet tall and live more than 2,000 years!

It's cool, dark, and very quiet as we wind our way around giant trunks growing so close to the highway that they reveal scrapes and scars of too close traffic. The only light that makes its way to the floor of this forest is first filtered through mists clinging to the branches and dripping dewdrops to the thirsty ferns far below. We pause in this ancient place, surrounded by peace and serenity.

Recently, a study done at the University of California Berkeley suggests trees may be in trouble because the coastal fog in Northern California and Oregon has decreased since the early twentieth century. The fog and the dew are vital to refresh and sustain these trees in times of drought.

∫∫∫

*The LORD says, "Then I will heal you of your faithlessness;*
*my love will know no bounds, for my anger will be*
*gone forever. I will be to Israel like a refreshing dew*
*from heaven. Israel will blossom like the lily;*
*it will send roots deep into the soil like the*
*cedars of Lebanon* (Hosea 14:4-5 NLT).

∫∫∫

Like these mighty trees, people can find themselves living a dewless life. Many people live their lives filled with anxiety, restlessness, and are too busy for God. We need to make a conscious effort to let go of those things which divert us from seeking and receiving God's sustaining and restoring love.

In God's Word, we find His promise of restoration from a burdened, heavy heart. We discover the glorious character of God, who is gracious. His love knows no bounds. We do not need to depend on the weather or on man for refreshing our weary soul. If we seek Him, we will be refreshed in His Holy Spirit, sending our roots to grow deep and strong, supporting us in the droughts of our life. We can depend on our eternal God. His blessings and His love will never dry up.

♪♪♪

"It is one of God's secrets. It comes quietly,
and yet works so mightily. We cannot produce
it, but we may receive it and live, moment by
moment, in that atmosphere where the Holy
Spirit may continually drench us with His presence."
—Pastor W. Mallis (*Springs in the Valley*, L. B. Cowman)

♪♪♪♪

# 33

## *Luminaries To The World*

The sun slipped off to hide behind the western foothills, while darkness spilled across the campground. Lanterns were lit, campfires crackled, and a bullfrog entertained the crowd with his solo song. Nestled on the edge of a large grassy field were a ragged line of various shaped and colored tents. As it grew dark, the tents glowed with the lanterns inside looking like pretty colored luminaries. One particular tent drew my attention and sparked my imagination.

Earlier that day, I walked down to the river, passing a bright yellow tent with its front flaps open. There sat a man on a little stool with a dog lying at his feet. The dog lifted its head and perked up his ears, watching as I passed. I tried not to stare at the quaint duo, but the man looked up and smiled warmly, tipping his broad brimmed hat in an old-fashioned greeting.

Now, this man's yellow tent seemed to glow, throwing a warm circle of light into the darkness. I thought of the words of Jesus and His gift of light to a dark world.

♪♪♪

*When Jesus spoke again to the people, he said,*
*"I am the light of the world. Whoever follows me*
*will never walk in darkness but will have*
*the light of life"* (John 8:12 NIV).

♪♪♪

This interesting fellow had a long white untrimmed beard. His head of white hair fell to his shoulders from under a safari-looking hat. His campsite was neat and tidy, giving the impression of one who had many years experience in setting up camp.

As I walked past his tent, I turned back to look again. I was surprised how the glowing lantern from in his tent threw his silhouette in perfect profile. Fascinated, I watched his shadow take on a larger than life expression of him and looking like an old time photo. The silhouette moved and I saw him bring a steaming mug up to his lips and juggle a large book on his lap.

Was that a Bible he held up when he waved to me earlier? With his friendly smile and a peace about him, there seemed to be an inner glow making me want to know more about him.

Our entire sufficiency is from Christ alone, not from ourselves. What others see is His presence in us. Like a warm smile, a nod of the head, and a lantern lit tent, we too can be luminaries to the world.

♪♪♪

"People are like stained glass windows; they sparkle and shine when the sun is out, but when the darkness sets in their true beauty is revealed only if there is a light within."
—Elizabeth Kubler-Ross

♪♪♪♪

# 34

## *Maggie's Legend*

I stood in the parking lot in front of our Beaver Valley Country Store, waving with one hand while holding a young mixed breed pup in the other. Watching my son and his friend drive away in his old jeep, heading for their summer in the mountains, I thought: Great, this dog is just what I need—one more responsibility, something else to take care of!

This dog was not going to be a large one, I could tell by her petite paws. She had long hair, large pointed ears, and a little fox like face. Maybe a sheltie and German shepherd mix? When she looked up at me with those big brown trusting eyes, I gave a reluctant sigh. I knew I was hooked.

Some weeks later, on one of those hectic busy summer days at the store, a customer came in the door laughing and said, "That's pretty smart of you, lady. That's quite a pup you have out there, very good for public relations for your store I'd say. Got any beef jerky I can buy her as a treat?"

"What do you mean public relations pup?" I asked.

"Well, I've never seen anything like it," he said. "That little dog looked up at me and smiled! Just as cute as you please! Made my day, and made me smile too. You know we all appreciate your place because you are always greeting us with a smile, but now even the dog smiles!"

∫∫∫

*"A cheerful look brings joy to the heart;*
*good news makes for good health"*
(Proverbs 15.30 NLT).

∫∫∫

80

Who would dream that one sorry pup could make people feel good? That dog really did smile! And her goofy smile melted many hearts and brought a million smiles back in return. Maggie became a legend. She ended up living with us for many years and she had her very own fan club. Maggie even received a letter once. It was addressed to: The Beaver Valley Country Store with the smiling dog out front. Only in the country and in a small town would the postmaster know where such a letter should be delivered!

Season after season people came in asking for Maggie. We'd call her out from her resting place behind the counter. Faithfully, she would wag her tail, and greet customers with her best doggie smile.

Tourists stopped by having heard about her from across the country! "Is the place with the smiling dog? We were told to stop and see her!"

God's Word teaches us the importance of cheerfulness. It's good for our disposition, our health, and our soul. It is one thing that we don't mind catching from someone else and it's okay to be contagious and pass it on.

♪♪♪

Who would believe one mutt dog could teach us the valuable lesson of how important a smile is? Even one from a dog! Though it's been nearly twenty years ago now and Maggie is in doggie heaven, people I meet will say, "You are the ones who had Maggie, the smiling dog!" Maggie's smiling legend lives on.

♪♪♪

"No one is useless in this world
who lightens the burden of another."
—Charles Dickens

♪♪♪♪

# 35

## *Measure By Measure*

I reached for my well-worn cookbook looking for directions to make a special treat for the family. Instead I decided to pull out the little three by five card file of my old and reliable recipes. I either knew these recipes by heart, or I had long forgotten what was even tucked into this little box. How long had I owned this collection of recipes? Could it be more than forty years now?

I picked a card that was dog-eared and stained, smiling as memories filled my heart. I could still see the person writing down this recipe. This was not just any recipe box. It was a treasure box of fond memories. With all of our new technology, I rarely write down recipes anymore. But here was a stained card with the thin, shaky script of my grandmother; another with the fluid and lovely handwriting of my mother; the neatly printed block letters of my best friend; and on it went. Each card showed the name of the person who shared what they believed to be a perfect recipe—worth the effort and worthy of praise.

I reflected on the baking lessons received from my mother. To mom, measuring made the difference between success and failure. My mother never had a failed creation that I could remember. Measuring meant success to her.

But my maternal grandmother rarely measured. The two women were opposite personalities when it came to cooking. Grandma went by memory, by touch, by smell. Her hands knew when more flour was needed, she tasted to see if salt was needed, and her nose told her when the baking was done. Each woman had a plan and an order to achieve their good results—they just went at it differently.

♪♪♪

*For this very reason, make every effort to add to your*
*faith goodness; and to goodness, knowledge; and to knowledge,*
*self-control; and to self-control, perseverance; and to*
*perseverance, godliness; and to godliness, brotherly kindness;*
*and to brotherly kindness, love. For if you possess these qualities*
*in increasing measure, they will keep you from being ineffective*
*and unproductive in your knowledge of our Lord*
*Jesus Christ* (2 Peter 1:5-8 NIV).

♫♫♫

Becoming Christ-like is a process, step-by-step, measure-by-measure. With self-discipline and a good heap of faith, we too will produce good character, good deeds, and a greater love for one another.

God's Word has the perfect recipe for success. No fear of putting in too much. Go ahead, heap-up that cup kindness, spill-over in godliness, knead-in more knowledge, and ladle-up more love. With faith and perseverance, we can always turn out a fine finished product.

♫♫♫

"The spiritual life and the love of God are
knit right into the texture of our lives."
—Leslie Williams

♫♫♫♫

# 36

## *Our Daily Hope*

One rainy afternoon I drove to a small, bayside Victorian town to attend a meeting. I parked my car nearby and noted I still had time for a quick lunch. It was Sunday afternoon and fall was splashing its way into town with every windswept rain drop. Not many places were open on this off season day, but I finally spotted a sign that said: "Climb the stairs and find the best cup of soup in town."

The little restaurant overlooking the bay was hushed, the voices of tourists long gone. The wait staff seemed happy and eager to have someone to serve. I was directed to the best little table in the place, right by the window overlooking the local ferry slipping along through the fog and rain. The smiling waitress came to my table with her hands full. One hand held a glass of water, a menu was tucked under her elbow, and the other hand held a basket of fresh hot bread.

I ordered my soup, pulled back the towel on the basket, and breathed in the wonderful aroma of thick-crusted bread. As I tore off a slice of the bread, I paused holding it before me, smiling, saying grace silently. I didn't care what others nearby thought, for my mind and heart were reflecting not on the bread alone, but on Jesus.

∫∫∫

*"I am the living bread that came down from heaven.
Anyone who eats this bread will live forever;
and this bread, which I will offer so the
world may live, is my flesh"*
(John 6:51 NLT).

♪♪♪

What a shocking message Jesus gave that day. Jesus wasn't speaking literally, of course. To eat "living bread" means to accept Christ into our lives and become united with Him. We are united with Jesus when we:
Believe in His death and resurrection;
Devote ourselves to living as He did;
Depend on God's Word to teach us; and
Trust His Holy Spirit to guide us.

When we eat our meals, when we hold our daily bread in our hands, we are reminded of His sacrifice for us. May we never see bread in the same way again, but rather see it as the bread of life, the bread of hope, the bread which sweetens, purifies, and is able to transform anyone.

♪♪♪

"While reason is puzzling itself about mystery,
faith is turning it to daily bread,
and feeding on it thankfully
in her heart of hearts."
—Frederic Dan Huntington

♪♪♪♪

# 37

## Patches Of God-Light

There is a place deep, deep in our forest that I love to visit in spring and summer. It's where I sense all around me the beauty and character of God. Stepping on the spongy moss forest floor, my footsteps are muffled as I tread my way to a quiet destination. I rest sitting on an ancient fallen "mother" cedar log.

I love this name given to fallen trees, for they never really die, but continually give birth to new growth as they sleep and slip back into the earth from where they began. This sleeping-beauty log is draped with a blanket of moss blooming with tiny white star-shaped flowers. As I rest upon the log I laugh thinking: I'm sitting on God's flower bed!

♪♪♪

*From the rising of the sun to the place where it sets,*
*the name of the* Lord *is to be praised* (Psalm 113:3 NIV).

♪♪♪

I love this verse about God's creation:

*"Among the gods there is none like You, O Lord; nor are there*
*any works like Your works. All nations whom You have made*
*shall come and worship before You, O Lord, and shall glorify*
*Your name. For You are great, and do wondrous things; You*
*alone are God"* (Psalm 86:8-10 NKJV).

I'm hidden in the hushed calm of God's sanctuary, filled with expectation that something wonderful is about to take place. The birds sing high above in the tree tops, blending into one sweet melodious song.

Though the sun rose on this stellar clear morning some time ago, I must wait hours for the sun to penetrate its way through the thick forest foliage. I sit holding my breath, waiting for the exact moment when I will see the first fingers of sunlight thread through and kiss the ferns good morning.

I watch the sun turn the dull green branches to a lustrous emerald green. Water droplets dangling from the tip of the hemlock, cedar, and great Sitka reflect the light, glimmering like a beautifully decorated Christmas tree. God-light has arrived once again.

Light is cast across the forest floor caressing the fiddle-head ferns, revealing incredible details rarely seen. Soon, beyond the human eye, the ferns will unroll and receive this brief life giving light, yawn, and go back to sleep.

♫♫♫

"We or at least I shall not be able to adore God on the brightest occasions if we have learned no habit of having so on the lowest. At best, our faith and reason will tell us that He is adorable, but we shall not have found Him so, not have 'tasted and seen.' Any patch of sunlight in a wood will show you something about the sun which you could never get from reading books on astronomy. These pure and spontaneous pleasures are "patches of God-light" in the woods of experience."

—C.S. Lewis

♫♫♫♫

# 38

## *The Path That Led To Fear*

This was our first time on this trail through the deep evergreen forest to our campground. We chatted happily, eager to get back to our camp. Our footsteps made no sound on the thick carpet of moss. The trees were so tall here the sun sent spokes of light through the branches. My fifteen-year-old brother, Dick, led the way, watching for the National Forest signs leading to our campsite.

We were so busy talking we didn't realize we could no longer see the lake through the trees. Where is our campsite set up? I nearly bumped into Dick when he stopped suddenly and said, "Sis, this path just ended!"

"What?" I said, walking around him to take a look. "What have we been following if not the path to the lake? Where is the next sign post?"

"Oh, I'm thinking it is a deer path, not a people path. And somewhere we missed a sign. I bet it rotted and fell down," he said in a soft and nervous voice.

∫∫∫

*"Don't be afraid, for I am with you. Don't be discouraged, for I am your God. I will strengthen you and help you. I will hold you up with my victorious right hand"* (Isaiah 41:10 NLT).

∫∫∫

When life seems to take us off our expected and planned paths and we find we have lost sight of the guideposts to direct us, fear trickles in us to undermine our confidence, clutter our minds, and sap our strength. But we need not let the fear become greater than our faith. Faith is the powerful stream of Living Water that quenches the flame of fear.

God has a promise that we can count on Him in every situation. His promise is to give us strength and direction in all circumstances, if we call on Him first—before we panic. We can trust God to do what He promises in our difficult times when we feel inadequate and with limited choices. We can count on God to be watching over us when we have lost our way. Dick and I stood there feeling fear rise, making us feel sick, stuck, frozen in place.

"What should we do?" he asked.

"Stopping is good," I say with a big sister smile. "But first take a deep breath, let's pray, and know that fear is our greatest enemy."

We turned around and took one tentative step at a time following the thin, nearly invisible deer path. We held hands and just kept on going, wondering if we were going the wrong way and deeper into the forest instead of back to the main path.

I took a step over a hump of fern and grass to get around a wet area. My toe stubbed something causing me to stumble and nearly fall. Dick started to yank it from the tangle of growth when I yelled, "Stop! Don't move it! It's the forest sign that fell down just like you said. We need to look and see which way the arrow is pointing to find our way out."

Even to me this sounded a bit crazy. But I felt strongly God was guiding us and this is what we needed to do. I silently prayed that when the sign had fallen, it hadn't twisted or turned and it still marked the way to go.

We looked at the arrow and then around us and made a slight turn to the left in the direction the arrow pointed. Soon the path became wider. In just a few more steps, we saw something that made us both shout! It was another Forest Service sign pointing towards our camp! We agreed we had experienced an extraordinary answer to prayer and an adventure with God we would never forget.

♫♫♫

"It is impossible for that man to despair
who remembers that his Helper is omnipotent."
—Jeremy Taylor

♫♫♫♫

# 39

## *Paying It Twice*

When I was living in Seattle, my Grandma Barr came to stay with me during Grandpa's surgery at the Veterans Hospital. The hospital was south of town from where I lived. I explained to Grandma it would take us two buses to get there. "Remember, when you pay to ask for a transfer ticket, there is no extra charge for that," I reminded her at the bus stop.

What I failed to ask Grandma was, "Do you have the correct change for the bus ride?" The drivers rarely had change for a large bill, even one larger than a five.

Grandma slowly made her way up the steep steps, gripping the handle for good measure. She juggled her purse and handed the bus driver a ten dollar bill!

I was still down on the bottom step looking up at her, wondering what was taking her so long when I heard the driver say, "Sorry, lady, I don't have enough change for that bill."

"What will I do? I'm from out of town, I didn't know this rule. I need to get to the hospital today to see my husband before he goes into surgery. Can I pay you on the way back? We will be coming on your bus again this afternoon," she asked innocently.

"I'm not likely to be your driver then. The odds of getting the same bus driver are pretty rare. Go on ahead now. Don't you worry. You go see your husband," the kind driver said.

"I will pay you, I promise. My yes is always a yes," my Grandmother declared.

∫∫∫

*My child, never forget the things I have taught you.*
*Store my commands in your heart. If you do this,*
*you will live many years, and your life will be satisfying.*
*Never let loyalty and kindness leave you!*
*Tie them around your neck as a reminder.*
*Write them deep within your heart.*
*Then you will find favor and both God and people,*
*and you will earn a good reputation*
(Proverbs 3:1-4 NLT).

♪♪♪

We made the long ride across town in time to see Grandpa before his surgery and see him doing well afterwards. We stopped for a little snack in the cafeteria and Grandma made sure she had small bills and coins. "I promised that nice driver I would pay up for my bus ride," I heard her say.

The bus hissed its way to the curb, the door swished open. As we began to climb on board, we were pleasantly surprised to see the same bus driver! "Well, if this isn't fate!" Grandma said, "Here you are young man, the two fares I owe you. And don't forget my transfer now."

Grandma was getting the hang of cross-city travel down pretty good.

"Well, I never thought I'd see you again today. At the last minute I had to put in an extra shift for someone who got sick. And I never, ever, thought I'd see you again, not to mention that you'd pay me on your way back—twice! Madame, you are making a believer out of me!"

That experience happened more than fifty years ago and it made a lifetime impression on me about keeping your word. It's a life principle I will never forget. Grandma walked the talk. Paying it twice left a long lasting legacy.

♪♪♪♪

# 40

## *Perfection In The Polishing*

When I was six years old, my mother and I lived across the street from a retired couple. Mrs. Balley I suspect knew I was often a lonely only child and would invite me to her home for high tea.

Mother and I lived in an older apartment building which was quite plain and simple compared to the Balley's quaint cottage-style home. My feet sank deep in the plush rose colored carpet. I loved the fragrance of lemon oil that had been rubbed faithfully into their beautiful old wood furnishings. Mrs. Balley greeted me at the front door and the tantalizing smell of fresh baked scones made my mouth water and my stomach growl with anticipation.

The tea set was on the table showcasing her delicate bone china cups and saucers, each with a little silver spoon to stir in the honey. I was honored to use a very a special cup and saucer which once was used by her daughter as a child. I wore my best dress, and remembered my mother's advice to wear my best manners. I watched every move Mrs. Balley made and copied every motion.

After tea time, Mr. Balley would come upstairs from his basement workshop and invite me to view his latest project. Mr. Balley was a skilled woodworker and I loved looking at the wooden toys he made.

One time on my visit to the basement, I heard a low rumbling noise coming from back in a dark corner of the room. "Mr. Balley," I asked, "what's that noise over there?"

"That, my friend, is a rock polisher," he said proudly.

For the life of me I couldn't understand why anyone would polish a rock. "My mother polishes our furniture, but we throw away any rocks that come in *our* house," I said. My tone of voice impling that rock polishing was just dumb.

"Come here. Let me show you what the rocks look like after they are polished. The rocks tumble around and around in sand for a long time before they are made into something special," he said.

He reached for a small box on the shelf and opened the lid to reveal the most beautiful rocks I had ever seen. They were no longer plain dirty rocks but beautiful to look at and smooth to touch.

"There are no two alike," Mr. Balley said, "Each has its own rare beauty, just like you. Look how they are rippled with gold, blue, and deep burnished browns. All that beauty was hidden until they were tumbled and polished for a long time."

♪♪♪

*So be truly glad. There is a wonderful joy ahead, even though you have to endure many trials for a little while. These trials will show that your faith is genuine. It is being tested as fire tests and purifies gold—though your faith is far more precious than mere gold. So when your faith remains strong through many trials, it will bring you much praise and glory and honor on the day when Jesus Christ is revealed to the whole world* (1 Peter 1:6-7 NLT).

♪♪♪

We all start out rough around the edges. But with every adversity God is perfecting us in our faith. The more friction, the more polishing going on, the more God can use us for His purpose.

I was allowed to choose one of those precious polished rocks as a reminder: There is beautiful perfection in the polishing.

♪♪♪

"The gem cannot be polished without friction nor the child of God perfected without adversity."
—Jeneanne Sieck (*Never Alone)*

♪♪♪♪

# 41

## *Praying For Others*

My husband, Bill, walked down to the aged, but neat and tidy trailer by the creek. His mission was to check on the renter who called saying he was suffering from lung cancer. This renter had always paid his rent on time for nearly fifteen years. But this time he'd made a rare phone call to us saying he just wasn't sure how he was going to be able to pay the rent in the future.

Bill knocked on the door. After a bit, he heard footsteps inside. He was surprised there was no barking of the man's old faithful shepherd dog. A few minutes later, the door creaked open and the renter's face poked out squinting from the bright sunshine.

Though the rent had come on a regular basis, personal contact and conversation had not. Bill realized he really knew very little about his renter. He did know that this man did an honest day's work out of the large attached shop, was a man of his word, and had a good reputation. Bill and I wondered: Does he have insurance? Does he know the Lord? How is he going to make it on his own, unable to do the small repairs that were his income?

### ∫∫∫

*Pray in the Spirit at all times and on every occasion.*
*Stay alert and be persistent in your prayers for*
*all believers everywhere* (Ephesians 6:18 NLT).

### ∫∫∫

We are urged to pray as individuals and together until victory is gained. Too often we are preoccupied with the needs of our family and loved ones. But we are reminded it is our responsibility to pray for others, even if we don't know them well, or even if they may not know the Lord.

Bill asked the renter if he could come in for a moment. There was a hesitation but slowly the door opened and he was invited inside. "Where's your dog today?" Bill asked.

It took a few minutes for the renter to answer. "He was up by the highway a few days ago, someone pulled over, stopped, opened their car door, and grabbed him then just drove away," he said choking back tears. "Now I've got cancer, can't work, and even my dog is gone." The sadness of this burden was so great that without thinking if he should or shouldn't, Bill asked, "Can I pray for you?"

The renter looked up and said, "Yes, *yes*, I would like that, sir."

Bill told the renter not to worry about the rent. He knew he had nowhere to go, things would work out, and just pay when and how he could. They parted with mutual respect and a warm and friendly handshake. A few days later, we were surprised to receive a call from the renter. This took some effort on the renter's part for he had no phone and had to walk to a neighbor's house to borrow one.

"Sir, I just wanted to thank you for that prayer the other day. Well you know, I just started feeling better about things right away. And just so you know, my friends came by yesterday and brought me a new dog. I also went and found a way to help pay the rent. I can tell you have a good heart, sir, thank you."

"It was my privilege friend. I will continue to pray for you," my husband answered.

We really were surprised by what the man said. It shows how much power there is in prayer and how showing a little love and concern goes a long way. The results are all up to God, but it really is an unspeakable joy to be able to pray for others. What a blessing to be in such union with Jesus that we are able to take part in His great work as intercessors and mingle our prayers with His.

♪ ♪ ♪

"May God help you to see what place intercession takes in His divine counsel and in the service of His kingdom. There is no greater honor or glory on earth than the privilege of intercession."
—Andrew Murray (*Daily in His Presence*)

∫∫∫∫

# 42

## *Pots With A Purpose*

I smiled at the woman waiting on me at a Hallmark store and said, "I really love your hair. The style fits you perfectly!" Her comment back to me was a bit surprising as she said, "I hate my hair! I have no idea why I got hair like this! It curls when I don't want it to, it won't stay put, and I fight it all the time!"

How odd, I thought, to me her hair fit perfectly on her oval face, flattered her big brown eyes, and announced a wonderful smile that seemed to fit her personality. Each was made for the other, as God created her to be. Yet, how like us all to struggle with ourselves to be something else rather than how God has made us.

∫∫∫

*What sorrow awaits those who argue with their Creator.*
*Does a clay pot argue with its maker?*
*Does the clay dispute with the one who shapes it,*
*saying, "Stop, you're doing it wrong!"*
*Does the pot exclaim, "How clumsy can you be?"*
*This is what the LORD says—the Holy One*
*of Israel and your Creator:*
*"Do you question what I do for my children?*
*Do you give me orders about the work of my hands?"*
(Isaiah 45:9, 11 NLT).

∫∫∫

We can only be who God designed us to be. There will be no others like us in the whole world. There aren't any two with the same fingerprints or DNA. Our mix of physical and personality features are unique to us. Why would God do this?

Why, because God's nature is to create, and design everything with great love—with a very specific purpose. God has a plan for our lives, a role in the world in each season, in every journey, in every trial, triumph, and adventure which we will face. With great hope and a deep appreciation for God's sovereignty, we can see how He created us for His purpose.

We were shaped inside and out, each with different abilities, aptitudes, personalities, and gifts. What may look odd and out of place to us according to the styles and cultures of this world—is to God a perfect fit for His purpose!

We may not see it in the mirror, but we can see it with our hearts when we read God's Word: Everything created by Him is made with His great love, filled with purpose, and is beautiful in His eyes. Every pot has a purpose; every person is perfected in His love.

♪♪♪

"The higher your view of God,
the higher the view of yourself."
—Jan Carlberg

♪♪♪♪

# 43

## *Second Chances*

I watched as my husband carefully laid out all the pieces and checked the instruction book at least twice before he started putting the new barbecue together. I personally would have opened the box, pulled out the parts, and just went for it. My way seems much more exciting, adds a bit of drama to one's life, and is a bit like doing a jigsaw puzzle without any picture to go by.

Ah, yes, well, this does backfire on me. There is one particular time I thought hand-hooking a rug would be fun. I went to the yarn shop, selected a rug kit, and impatiently listened as the clerk tried to give me detailed directions and explain the process.

"Just show me how to use that cutter thingy and how to work the hook to loop the yarn, I'll be fine," I said.

∫∫∫

*Listen to my instruction and be wise.*
*Don't ignore it* (Proverbs 8:33 NLT).

∫∫∫

The minute I got home I eagerly took out my project and tossed the instructions aside. I liked the pretty design in the center of the rug, so I picked up the matting and that's where I began. Blissfully, I hooked around and around in the center of the rug until I noticed an odd thing: I was out of yarn!

"Wait a minute, that can't be right," I muttered to myself. "It's all pre-measured to complete the project, and I only have the middle of the rug done! They made a mistake!"

Mother's words came back to haunt me, "You'll paint yourself into a corner without planning your project."

The next week I strolled into the yarn shop and asked the same clerk for more yarn. "I'm a bit put out that there was a mistake in the kit you sold me, and now I have to spend more money to complete it."

"Out? How can you be out of yarn? That's never happened before, ever. Please bring the rug in and let me take a look at it for you. Let's see if we can figure out what might have gone wrong," she said a bit flustered.

ʃ ʃ ʃ

*The wise are glad to be instructed, but babbling fools*
*fall flat on their faces* (Proverbs 10:8 NLT).

ʃ ʃ ʃ

Wisely I said nothing more and returned the next day with my project in hand. The mystery was soon obvious.

"You began to hook your rug in the center, when you should have begun up here in the top left hand corner and done it row by row," the clerk said kindly.

"Not around and around?" I mumbled, quite humbled.

With much grace, the clerk did not say one critical word. She helped me pick out enough yarn to finish the rug and said, "Let's give you a second chance here. I'll only charge you half price for the extra yarn you need. One thing for sure, the center of your rug will never ever wear out."

She was right, that rug is still around today, fifty years later!

For a long time I tried to live my life my way without seeking God's Word, His directions for our life. And I have made many foolish choices. I've learned the hard way to first read all the directions of any project. In my personal life, I thank my loving Father for his forgiveness of those poor choices I made.

We are able to come to Jesus and ask forgiveness for those very big and serious mistakes, and bring to Him the threads of every small one. With His unfailing love and complete forgiveness, with no condemnation for our mistakes, He offers freely a second chance to begin again.

♪♪♪

"Very often what God first helps us towards is not the virtue itself but just this power of always trying again."
—C.S. Lewis

♪♪♪♪

# 44

## *Skinny Kid And A Fat Tire Bike*

Several of us were comparing our childhood birthdays the other day. For me, my favorite birthday was the year I turned seven. It was the birthday I didn't get what I expected. What I hoped for was a two wheel bike. I watched with envy as my 1950's childhood friends zipped around the neighborhood and to school on their slim and sleek Schwinn bikes. Why some even had handbrakes!

It took two years for my friend, Bobby Stray's brother, to buy one from what he earned on his paper route. I knew this was an expensive gift for our family, but I had talked a blue streak on how this particular bike would last me all the way through high school!

The big day for my birthday party arrived. I was waiting with great anticipation for the sleek red bike to arrive. But the party was nearly over and I thought there was to be no bike for me this year, when my Dad walked in saying, "You better come outside and see what was just delivered from Sears."

There it was! A bike, a big—blue bike with big fat tires! First, I was happy. Then I felt ashamed. I didn't feel grateful. All I felt was disappointed. I thought of peddling that big heavy bike around like a slug, while the rest of the kids would be zooming by me. I'd never have a chance to win a race now.

"What kind of bike is this?" I asked.

"It's a B.F. Goodrich bike, and it will last you a long, long time," my parents said proudly. "This bike is made for endurance."

∫∫∫

*Dear brothers and sisters, when troubles come your way,*
*consider it an opportunity for great joy. For you know*
*that when your faith is tested, your endurance has*
*a chance to grow. So let it grow, for when your*
*endurance is fully developed, you will be*
*perfect and complete, needing*
*nothing* (James 1:2-4 NLT).

♪♪♪

I was in turmoil. I had grateful feelings for what my family had done for me. But I was also feeling embarrassed because no one I knew had a fat-tire bike!

Quickly, I learned to ride my bike. To my surprise, I was a fast and furious competitor. Then I discovered a funny thing one day, I didn't care anymore that my bike was blue, and didn't have handbrakes or gears. I didn't care it was a big fat tire bike.

Because of its size and weight I was developing stronger muscles and an incredible endurance. I was fearless, challenging both girls and boys to race me. I shot right past the other kids on their lightweight bikes and I rarely got winded! I could peddle faster to the park, be waiting for them at the corner store, streak up steep hills, and slam on that foot break with great precision. Who would have thought?

That old B.F. Goodrich bike lasted me into my early teen years. Then I passed it on to my siblings. I didn't know what a special gift I received that birthday. I didn't know it was going to be more than just a bike—it was going to be good for me!

It was a lifetime lesson I learned that year. About how God may ask you to: make-do with what you have; learn to peddle hard against all adversity; and be surprised at the endurance you will have to win the race—even if you're only a skinny kid on a fat-tire bike.

♪♪♪

Lord, there's so much wisdom to be learned,
So many ways for me to grow.
I pray I would listen and learn like a child
All that You would have me know.
—Dee Kamp

♪♪♪♪

# 45

## *Songs From The Fire*

Have you sat around a crackling, snapping campfire or in front of a fireplace and found yourself listening to the fire hiss and sing? The wood used for a good long-lasting fire is a big chunk of wood we call "the back log." The rest is kindling which will burn up hot and quickly disappear.

When the back log catches fire it often begins to make a multitude of melodic sounds. When the snapping and crackling of the fire slows down, there is a whistling, squeaking, even a flute like sound coming from the back log.

Often the room grows quiet and everyone seems drawn to listen to its music, the songs of the forest fill the room. The log sings from the memories of the song birds in spring, the hoot of the owl at night, the flute like sound of the tree frog chirping after the rain. The tree's songs are recalled from its memory of when the high winds blew strumming through its branches and the sound of the hissing snow and sleet in a harsh winter storm.

♪♪♪

*But the people of God will sing a song of joy,*
*like the songs  at the holy festivals.*
*You will be filled with joy,*
*as when a flutist leads a group of pilgrims*
*to Jerusalem, the mountain of the* LORD—
*to the Rock of Israel* (Isaiah 30:29 NLT).

♪♪♪

It's a writer's fancy to hear songs of the forest singing from a sizzling log in the fire. But it is a bit of a parable of our lives. Each of us has collected many songs from our own lives over the years.

Some of the best songs remembered are the ones resulting from the times we were "in the fire" of life's trials. Some people may never learn to sing until the flames kindle a memory deep within them.

When struggles come and go, we know God strengthens us to endure them. Let us then let the flames of our passion release the captured songs in our heart. These songs and melodies have been stored away to sing praises to our God for all He has done for us. It's the songs from the fire that are most effective, most remembered, and most beautifully sung.

♪♪♪

"Many a rejoicing Christian never learned
To sing till the flames kindled upon him."
—J. R. Miller (*Springs in the Valley*)

♪♪♪♪

# 46

## *Source From A Higher Place*

It is an artesian well and you won't ever need to put down a pump to get your water. You're lucky that way," our neighbor told us about our purchase of a Beaver Valley Country Store. Because we were city folks when we bought the store, we had a lot to learn.

The friendly and supportive locals were third and fourth generation families, who had established the farms, fished the waters, and logged the forest around us. They were light years ahead of us when it came to both experience and good country sense.

I stood by the well and stared down at it, realizing I had no idea what was meant by an "artesian well." I was still trying to get the hang of country living. Now I had visions of an old wishing well in my head.

"Am I going to have to pull this water up by the bucket full to make coffee for our customers? Is there enough pressure to bring the water into the store year around?" I asked.

The kindly man did his best to hide his laughter. "Your supply, your source of water, comes from a higher place. This means this well is drilled deep enough to reach water that is draining down from a higher piece of ground. In your case, the mountain pressure will force the water to flow upward with a natural pressure of its own. The pipes that are going inside the store have plenty of fresh good water and enough pressure to give you more than you'll ever need. That well has been faithfully working now for more than fifty years."

∫∫∫

*Such things were written in the Scriptures long ago*
*to teach us. And the Scriptures give us hope*
*and encouragement as we wait patiently*
*for God's promises to be fulfilled*
(Romans 15:4 NLT).

♪♪♪

Relying on the promises of God's Word affects how we live, lifts our spirits, and like the artesian well is our source of strength from a higher place. All the Living Water we will ever need is available and free for the asking. With God we can depend on a never ending supply of fresh hope and faith to sustain us all the days of our lives.

♪♪♪

"Hope—that bubbling ingredient in life
which is like carbonation in a drink—giving it zest,
keeping it in motion, is always pushing it up."
—Max DePree

♪♪♪♪

# 47

## *Spring Cleaning The Heart*

Today is the perfect day for spring cleaning! It's a day to throw open the windows of our heart and let God's Spirit flow through refreshing the staleness that gathered there. Pull away the curtains hanging heavy on your heart. Shake away the dust of regret and dullness of despair with fresh new hope.

God sent His Son, Jesus, as our cleansing solution for tough stains. He is our hope on a rope to wash and shine away our heavy burdens. Oh, let us be swept free and unfettered in a new season of faith!

♪♪♪

*Create in me a clean heart, O God.*
*Renew a loyal spirit within me*
(Psalm 51:10 NLT).

♪♪♪

God wants us to be happy from inside out. When Jesus was born in Bethlehem the angels shouted "Joy to the World!" Love came down the stairway of heaven, and Hope was born for all mankind. We are no longer captive to our sin. We never again need to settle for long winters in our souls.

The joy of the Lord is our strength! Jesus promises to rekindle the dim light of hope in us, with new compassion every morning, forgiveness forever. He longs to lavish us with His endless supply of love.

Come, it's time to dust off the limiting lint of the past, to unclog the air vent of the heart that gave us that fuzzy view of Jesus and paralyzed our relationship with Him.

If we ask, He will help us to let go of what's gone wrong, and give us a Holy Spirit power-wash to spring clean our heart.

♪♪♪

*Soak me in your laundry and I'll come out clean,*
*scrub me and I'll have a snow-white life.*
*Tune me in to foot-tapping songs,*
*set these once-broken bones to dancing.*
*Don't look too close for blemishes,*
*give me a clean bill of health.*
*God, make a fresh start in me,*
*shape a Genesis week from*
*the chaos of my life*
(Psalm 51:7-15 The Message).

♪♪♪♪

# 48

## *Spiritual Balance*

The crunch on the gravel caused me to pause from my morning coffee and look to see who might be coming down our road so early. What I see pulls at my heartstrings and makes me laugh.

On a shiny new two-wheel bike is a little boy about five-years-old peddling awkwardly and gripping the handlebar with all his might. He is leaning precariously to his right fighting for balance. The only thing holding the boy up and preventing his fall is the young man running alongside him and hanging on for dear life. This little guy is oblivious to the efforts of his strong daddy helping him keep his balance.

∬∬∬

*Show me the path where I should walk, O Lord;*
*point out the right road for me to follow.*
*Lead me by your truth and teach me,*
*for you are the God who saves me.*
*All day long I put my hope in you.*
(Psalm 25:4-5 NLT).

∬∬∬

Though the child cannot see his father behind him, he is confident his daddy is there and won't let him fall. Many of us can relate to being that child. Later in life, we've been the nervous and excited parent watching our child take a big step in growing up.

Sounds a lot like God doesn't it? Like the beginner on the bike, there are times we are striving to keep our balance. We have days when we feel like it's the first time we have ever tried to ride a bike.

No matter one's age or the miles they've gone, life still presents endless new lessons and plenty of challenges.

Our Father in heaven is like that daddy holding up the child until he gets his balance. The Lord helps us keep our balance in a world turned upside down. His Word reminds us He is faithful and trustworthy to hold us up, pick us up, and help us up when we crash and fall.

Good balance is important. And faith in God for spiritual balance is vital to keep peddling down the road.

♪♪♪

"The Christian journey is the process of learning to accept
Christ's outstretched hand as he leads us down
the sometimes mucky road of life."
—Leslie Williams

♪♪♪♪♪

# 49

## *Swinging Bridges*

Marching along two-by-two, my family and I followed the narrow path. Soon we could hear the rushing of waters and feel the air became cooler. It felt as though we were misting our faces with a spray bottle. We paused as my father began to speak.

"There is a surprise for you up ahead. I have saved it until now. You are going to cross over a deep cavern with a fast running river on a swinging bridge," he announced in a booming voice filled with excitement.

I froze unable to take one more step as the words "swinging bridge" swirled around in my brain. Our father went on to educate us as he read the brochure about this amazing man-made wonder.

"Capilano Suspension bridge was built in 1889 by a Scotchman, George Mackay. It is 450 feet across and two hundred and thirty feet above the Capilano Canyon with the Capilano River rushing through it."

*♪♪♪*

*"Yes, come," Jesus said. So Peter went over the side of the boat and walked on the water toward Jesus. But when he saw the strong wind and the waves he was terrified and began to sink. "Save me, Lord!" he shouted* (Matthew 14:29-30 NLT).

*♪♪♪*

Peter believed Jesus and had enough faith to step out of the boat. But Peter allowed the powerful wind and wild waves to distract him and he took his eyes off Jesus. It was then Peter realized his weaknesses and knew—it was impossible.

Can you imagine Peter thinking something like, "What was I thinking?" Peter forgot that it did not depend on him to stay on top of the water, but it was through faith in Jesus.

When we tread on troubled waters, let us not for one minute take our eyes off of Jesus. If we allow our minds to wander to measure the size of the danger, then our faith will take a plunge.

Jesus understood Peter's switch of focus to himself. With great love and compassion, Jesus held out His outstretched hand to Peter, just as He holds it out to us today.

I was dismayed watching my little brothers run boldly—with no fear at all—across the bridge. I gripped the railing, looked down, and nearly sat down to steady myself. But my Dad strongly encouraged me to look up and not down and keep going.

It was hard not to do the opposite of what I was being told. After all, that's where the danger was—down. But I realized that "up" was where my faith came from to succeed. And that's what I did. I trusted wisdom over fear and made it across, not once—but twice!

♪♪♪

"Not by measuring the waves can you prevail; not by
gauging the wind will you grow strong; to scan the danger
may be to fall before it; to pause at the difficulties, is to
have them break above your head. Lift your eyes unto the
hills, and go forward—there is no other way."
—L. B. Cowman (*Streams in the Desert*)

♪♪♪♪

# 50

## *Those Car Wash Experiences*

Shoving the coin into the slot of the commercial car wash, I choose option three. Option three is the shortest time it takes for my car to be scrubbed clean. Why I experience such dread of going through a car wash, I cannot rationalize. To be closed up in my car with no choice but to be stuck in there, and to have my car move on the conveyer belt without being able to control it myself, makes me nervous.

Next, I am made nearly deaf by the roaring sound of blasting water jets. Then, I duck as my car is being slapped by huge wiggly flapping things. It simply sets my teeth on edge every time. Perhaps I need car wash therapy! Obviously, I don't do this often enough because I have little faith that I will emerge safe and shiny bright on the other side.

∫∫∫

*But now, O Jacob, listen to the Lord who created you.
O Israel, the one who formed you says, "Do not be afraid, for
I have ransomed you. I have called you by name; you are mine.
When you go through deep waters, I will be with you.
When you go through rivers of difficulty, you will not drown.
When you walk through the fire of oppression, you
will not be burned up; the flames will not consume
you. For I am the Lord, your God the Holy One
of Israel, your Savior"* (Isaiah 43:1-3 NLT).

∫∫∫

During those times in life when we feel like we are on a conveyor belt of bad circumstances, and we feel we are the victim rather than vindicated, God promises He will give us strength and hope to make it through to the other side.

In Isaiah, God's love is so powerfully established. God never breaks a promise. His Word is the truth. His truth will set us free from our fears.

♫♫♫

*"First I predicted your rescue, then I saved you and proclaimed it to the world ... From eternity to eternity I am God.*
*No one can snatch anyone out of my hand.*
*No one can undo what I have done"*
(Isaiah 43:12-13 NLT).

♫♫♫

In the tunnel of my despair, in the fear of deep waters, I am able to remain calm and confident—counting my blessings for all the times God has been there for me. He has rescued me time after time from all my "car wash experiences."

♫♫♫

How wonderful to know that God
Watches us from above
And He will always shelter us in
His ever-present love!
—Dee Kamp

♫♫♫♫

# 51

## *Trustworthy Crossing Guard*

Two second grade girls held hands as they always did on their walk to school. They were best friends from the first day they met in kindergarten. Now ever since that day, they could be seen skipping along on their "never step on a crack or break your mother's back" pathway to school.

But this morning they were nervous and afraid. On this day in October on the way to school, the street lights were still on but barely shining through the thick fog. The power lines buzzed eerily, dripping heavy drops of moisture on their heads as they hurried by.

"How will we see to cross the street at school?" Della asked worriedly.

"Don't worry," Mary said, "You know Mr. Webber, our crossing guard, will be there to help us. I'm pretty sure anyway."

They continued on staring straight ahead, but still not able to see left, right, above, or ahead of them. Disembodied voices floated around them and they could hear the swish-swish of cars driving by, but oddly they couldn't see them at all. (Later it would be reported, this was the foggiest day in history and visibility was zero!)

The girls stopped, sensing the end of the sidewalk, and balanced the toe of their shoes at the edge of the curb. This is it—the big school crossing. Where is the guard? All they could see was swirling fog.

ʃ ʃ ʃ

*You see me when I travel and when I rest at home.*
*You know everything I do. You know what I*
*am going to say even before I say it, LORD.*
*You go before me and follow me.*
*You place your hand of blessing on my head.*
*Such knowledge is too wonderful for me,*
*too great for me to understand!*
(Psalm 139:3-6 NLT).

♪♪♪

A voice called to them from the darkness, "Come on girls, its okay. Come on now, I've got the traffic stopped for you."

Still the girls didn't move, where was the voice coming from? "We can't see you, Mr. Webber!"

"Just because you can't see me, doesn't mean I can't see you. Now take one step at a time and follow my voice, I'll keep talking, don't be afraid."

Hesitantly, the girls took small steps onto the road, still unable to see Mr. Webber. They stopped with a jerk, feeling a hand tapping them on the top of their heads!

"There, there. See, here I am. Now take my hand and I will take you the rest of the way."

There will be times when we feel God is far from us and we can't see Him working in our lives. But that is not true. God is exactly where He needs to be, right beside us. God has not moved away from us, perhaps we have moved away from Him.

God's chief desire is to reveal Himself to us. His touch is so delightful, that we are delightfully drawn to Him. We can always depend on God's promise that no matter the weather, no matter where in the world we are, God knows exactly where to find us. He will help us cross every road, climb every mountain, and walk through every valley. God is our loving, trustworthy crossing guard.

♪♪♪

"God's love for you is unflappable:
His presence unstoppable."
—Jan Carlberg

♪♪♪♪

# 52

## *Unlimited Dreams*

Buckets swinging in their hands, the two little boys dashed with delight into the gentle rolling waves of the ocean. There they bent down to scoop the buckets with more water for their sand castle. For boys so young it was amazing how hard they worked, running back and forth from sea to shore with tireless effort.

Now and then they would stop and stare at the grand castle coming into shape by the hands of their daddy. Little sister and mother found, scraps of driftwood, shells, and a feather for the finishing touches. (Women, it seems, are always into decorating and feathering their nests.)

"Hurry," I heard their father call. "The tide is coming in!"

I worried the boys didn't fully understand what their dad meant. Did they know their work to build this castle would eventually result in it all being washed away in seconds?

∫∫∫

*"Anyone who listens to my teaching and follows it is wise,
like a person who builds a house on solid rock. Though the
rain comes in torrents and the floodwaters rise and the winds
beat against the house, it won't collapse because it is built
on bedrock. But anyone who hears my teaching and ignores
it is foolish, like a person who builds a house on sand.
When the rains and floods come and the winds beat
against that house, it will collapse with a
mighty crash"* (Matthew 7:24-27 NLT).

∫∫∫

Of course, the children knew it was a game. I could see the family laughing and glancing back and forth at the incoming tide, yelling and shouting encouragement to each other to hurry up. This was a cooperative game to see if they could construct their castle and let it stand long enough to take a picture before it would wash away.

And they did just that. Mother took a photo of them proudly standing beside their castle with the feather flying from the highest turret, just as the tide was rushing about their feet, filling the moat and claiming the castle for its own.

Jesus spoke in terms the men and women about Him could understand. It is advice for all generations: When we want to build something, whether it is a house, castle, or basis for life, we'd better not build on sand. Jesus is the Rock, the foundation that will support and stand forever: All other options will fail.

When our faith is like that of a small child, Jesus will guide us and bless our efforts. Then and only then will we know our lives, our relationships, our faith can stand the tests of time. With God we are blessed with unlimited dreams to be built on His sure foundation.

♪♪♪

"Devotion to God is not limited to certain times
or occasions. It is always alive and stirring
in our thoughts, will desires, and affections.
If we are all called to this inward holiness
and goodness, then a perpetual working of the
Spirit of God within us is absolutely necessary."
—Andrew Murray (*Daily in His Presence*)

♪♪♪♪

# 53

## *Wind of God*

A stagnate air alert has been posted in our area again. The weather bureau suggests if you have breathing problems, stay indoors. Air stagnation occurs when an air mass remains over an area for an extended amount of time. To remove stagnant air from our environment, we need wind and rain to clear the air again.

∫∫∫

*For the Spirit of God has made me, and the breath of the Almighty gives me life* (Job 33:4 NLT).

∫∫∫

As God's people, when we pray we breathe cleaner air and we are healthier because of it. Praying allows us to have a breath of Godly fresh air filling us with insight and discernment to help us make wise decisions.

When we turn all our thoughts and deeds to ourselves, we become stuffy and stale. The air seems too thick and heavy to breathe comfortably. Our souls thirst and cry out for a fresh wind, a sweet breeze.

We may wonder why we are so unsatisfied, depressed, and restless. We feel as if our breath has been squeezed from us. This is when God may be sending us a stagnant air report.

Praying the Scriptures (God's Word) back to Him blesses us by receiving His cleansing air from heaven to renew our spirits and remove the stale air from stagnated thoughts, indifference, and idle ideas.

As Christians, we have great hope in God's promises for His unfailing love, cleansing waters, and pure heavenly air to breathe.

When we pray, we receive a refreshing wind of God that allows Him to reign in our hearts once again.

We may need to check the weather report for the air stagnation for our breathing concerns here on earth, but all we need to be refreshed in our spirit is the heartfelt prayer. The wind of God will give us hope and strength to sail through our day.

♫♫♫

"Wind of God, blow through me
Wind of God,
Come and set my spirit free
I raise my sail
And I won't move until
The wind of God
Blows through me."
—Bob Rose

♫♫♫♫

# The Stories Index

# Beaver Valley
## Country Store Stories Index

*(Stories written by Dee from her time in Beaver Valley on Highway 19, in Jefferson County, near Port Ludlow, Washington)*

# About the Author

Dee Kamp began writing while struggling to come to grips with the tragic death of her only son, Howard. Her husband, Bill, bought her a new Women's Bible and said read. Her best friend bought a journal and said write what you feel, what you see, what you experience. She has not stopped doing either for the past fifteen years.

"What I discovered was that God wasn't just up there somewhere, He was in every aspect of my life. He opened the eyes of my heart to His Word, and then He began to completely change me from seeing only misery to seeing His miracles. God made me aware it was His gifts of strength, hope, love, and even laughter that got me through my darkest days and deepest valleys," Dee says.

What looked to many people like coincidences in her life, God showed Dee that they were His divine appointments. As Dee began to look back in her life, even as a small child, she could see God had been there.

Who could explain the hard times, failures, and even dangerous episodes turned into successes? These life stories inspired her to write and share them with other women to uplift and encourage them in God's Word.

Four years ago she began sending weekday email inspirational messages called "His Word" to family, then friends, and the list of readers continues to grow today.

Dee makes her home in Port Ludlow, Washington, with her husband Bill. They enjoy being active in their church, as well as time spent with their children, grandchildren, and extended family members spread across the United States.

## To Contact The Author
## For Speaking Engagements,
## Book Orders, And Your Comments —

Dee's first booklet was published in 1998 and has had three printings:

*His Word: New Every Morning* (Grace Every Morning Ministries, 193 Seattle Drive, Port Ludlow, Washington 98365 U.S.A).

If you have enjoyed this book, **Strength for Today, Hope for Tomorrow,** or if it has had an impact on your life, we would like to hear from you. Please contact:

Dee Kamp
Grace Every Morning Ministries
~~193 Seattle Drive~~
~~Port Ludlow, Washington 98365 USA~~
Email: deekamp1@gmail.com

To contact the author about speaking, to order additional books, or to receive her daily e-mail meditations, email Dee Kamp at: deekamp1@gmail.com.

Breinigsville, PA USA
03 January 2011
252587BV00004B/3/P